385.72 llueb

52 Things Brides on a Budget Should Know

For Brian, Sophie, and Max, the most magical, inspiring family I could ever wish for. Thanks for always bringing out the best in me.

52 Things Brides on a Budget Should Know

Aimee Manis

TRADE PAPER
PRESS

Turner Publishing Company
200 4th Avenue North • Suite 950
Nashville, Tennessee 37219
(615) 255-2665

www.turnerpublishing.com

52 Things Brides on a Budget Should Know

Copyright © 2010 Turner Publishing Company

Library of Congress Cataloging-in-Publication Data

Manis, Aimee.
 52 things brides on a budget should know / Aimee Manis.
   p. cm.
 ISBN 978-1-59652-593-1
 1. Weddings--Planning. I. Title. II. Title: Fifty-two things brides on a budget should know.
 HQ745.M316 2010
 395.2'2--dc22
                    2010025592

Printed in China

10 11 12 13 14 15 16 17—0 9 8 7 6 5 4 3 2 1

*I dreamed of a wedding of elaborate elegance, a church filled with family and friends.
I asked him what kind of a wedding he wished for, he said one that would make me his wife.*
~Anonymous

Contents

Introduction   *xv*

The 52 Things   *1*

1. Budget common sense—it's not so common   *3*

2. Otherwise engaged: setting the date   *21*

3. Location, location, location   *27*

4. Your wedding style: it can look luxe for less   *45*

5. The reception (or, Why rubber chicken eats up your budget)   *55*

6. Entertainment: it can make or break your party   *77*

7. Frugalista florals: snobbery will get you nowhere   *83*

8. Down the aisle in style: your dress and accessories   *99*

9. Wedding photography is always worth the splurge   *125*

10. Paper artistry: invitations and stationery   *139*

11. Wedding favors: say it with sugar   *151*

12. Bridesmaids gifts: choose personality over price   *159*

13. Bridal beauty: when to go pro   *165*

14. Haute honeymoons with hot deals   *181*

Conclusion   *189*

Notes   *192*

Introduction

Introduction

As I sit down to begin writing this book, I realize that I have been to and written about hundreds of weddings. Weddings that, for the most part, were outrageously extravagant events that cost more than most of us would spend on several years' worth of rent, or on a car, or for the down payment on a first house. For many years, it seemed that weddings were being paid for with Monopoly money, where prices on everything from the reception food to the wedding gown were set at whim, and where couples were willing to pay exorbitant amounts of money without nearly the blink of an eye. We're talking weddings where the entire 300 guests were paraded through Beverly Hills on horse-drawn carriages between the church and the reception site and weddings where each female guest took home a pair of Chopard sapphire earrings and each male guest left with a pair of platinum cuff links. Not to mention the brides that spent a king's ransom on months of diamond dust facials, sunlit highlights painted on by Frederic Fekkai himself, and wedding gowns that may as well have been lined in five-hundred-dollar bills for the price. Monopoly money, right?

And now, as I'm writing, the tide has changed. I suppose the economy is just simple physics, the theory that what goes up must come down. It wasn't that long ago that conspicuous consumption couldn't get more conspicuous (designer logo-emblazoned water-bottle holders, anyone?), and now, not only are people shying away from bold excess and declaring it in bad taste, they are actually feeling guilty when they do overindulge. We're all bombarded with evidence of global warming, world poverty, and selfishness on a daily basis. (Thank you, Oprah.) The general movement toward appreciating things that are meaningful and lasting in life is spilling over into wedding planning as well. Whether you choose to embrace the trend of having a "green" wedding, in all of its wastefulness-shunning glory, you'll no doubt take notice of its budget-based and equally prudent sibling: the simple and authentic wedding. I, for one, am thrilled at this "new" wedding style. Whether you have a few thousand dollars to spend on your wedding or a budget of many times that, weddings are gradually becoming more of a reflection of the couple, their personalities, and their values than a reflection of their bank balance. And because you're reading this book, I'll assume that you have certain financial limitations for your wedding, and that's much less of a challenge than it once was. I know that may seem hard to believe, but now more than ever, there is an open-mindedness regarding weddings that embraces the unique and encourages creativity. There are so many ways that you can trim costs of your wedding without sacrificing style or compromising your vision of your day, ways that none of your guests will ever notice otherwise. And I'm here to tell you how to do just that.

You have my word: I won't pressure you into anything that I wouldn't have done at my own wedding. For example, if your wish is to have six bridesmaids, I'm not going to insult your intelligence by declaring that you should only have one so you can save money on bouquets and bridesmaids gifts (even though, um, it is true), nor will I advise you to have a cash bar at your reception (would you invite someone into your home and then charge them for a mojito?). I'm also not going to tell you that decorating with helium balloons is a fabulous and stylish alternative to fresh flowers: they're not. Why play games here? And I won't even resort to that now-familiar admonishment to overzealous brides everywhere: remember, it's just one day! Yeah, yeah, we know.

Nor will I tell you what amount you should spend on your flowers or your wedding gown. You're an adult. (Well, I hope you're over eighteen, anyway.) There are a million books and wedding Web sites that will give you itemized budget lists and calculate percentages for you based on the total amount you have to spend. I'm not going to waste space here telling you that you have to pay for your marriage license, that you should spend exactly 2 percent of your total budget on your bridal gown, and that you should remember to budget for your wedding rings. Let's assume that if you're mature enough to become betrothed, you're not clueless.

What I will share with you is many of the insider tips I've seen brides successfully use time after time, tips that will help ensure your wedding is as meaningful, memorable, and blessed as you can imagine—and cost less than you'd thought was possible. Whenever I tell someone about my career in the wedding industry, they always want to know just how over-the-top my own wedding was, and they are stunned when they find out that it wasn't like that at all. When pressed, I say, "Well, I guess it was pretty simple . . . uncontrived . . . low-key . . . maybe you'd call it modern traditionalist?" The interesting part is that I don't consider myself that much of a traditionalist, I don't live for being the center of attention, and I wasn't even completely married to the idea of a full-on wedding at all. I would have been perfectly content to exchange vows on the beach in bare feet, with a guest total I could count on one hand, followed by a magnificent honeymoon. It's not that I didn't love all of the gorgeously produced weddings I attended, it just didn't feel necessary. On the other hand, my husband had a very traditional point of view. He wanted a religious ceremony, witnessed by as many close friends and family as possible, followed by the champagne toasts, the mother-son dances, the mammoth wedding cake— the whole package. Because it meant a tremendous amount to him, I swayed to his dream blueprint of the day as much as I could without caving into the whole bigger-is-better mindset that was still going strong at that time (2001). So how did we find our middle ground?

After watching so many friends and clients butt heads over wedding details, I realize how fortunate my husband and I were to create something totally personal that fit the distinctive visions each of us had. I would be downplaying the whole process if I said that we simply compromised, because to me a compromise implies that one of the two people is losing something. Rather than going down our wish list saying, "Okay, fine, you get to have that massive, triple-tiered cake, but it ain't gonna be white fondant," we mapped out the key elements of the wedding, from the date and location down to the flowers, menu, and everything else, and discussed what things were most important to us. Fortunately for us, most of the facets that we didn't agree on didn't cause much drama. It seemed that each element was significant to only one of us, and the other didn't care quite as much and didn't mind giving in on that particular issue. That's how we ended up getting married by a rabbi, but in front of only 75 guests instead of the 200 friends that my husband had considered vital . . . and how we danced the hora, but it was played by a salsa band . . . oh yeah, and how we did, in fact, have a giant wedding cake, but I made sure it was chocolate, and square, and covered in candied fruits with not a drop of fondant in sight. It was all so beautiful, and it was us. Somehow, we each got the wedding that we wanted and nothing that we didn't.

I suppose that in my next life, I will insist on an uber-chic unwedding, an intimate party in some swanky supper club where I can wear an exquisite midnight blue cocktail dress, and serve a coconut cheesecake and vodka gimlets. And, of course, still take that fantastic honeymoon afterwards.

I hope that *52 Things Brides on a Budget Should Know* will keep you from feeling trapped by your budget constraints and will help you avoid the temptation to spend on things that are unnecessary as well as make sure you don't spend money on things you're not even excited about. These 52 Things, or tips, are found within the fourteen chapters, each to help you discover ways to cut costs and budget properly. If there's one thing you should know for sure after reading *52 Things,* it's that you don't have to go into debt to have an incredibly special, stylish, and chic wedding.

The 52 Things

~ 1 ~
Budget common sense—it's not so common

— 1 —

Budget common sense—it's not so common

If you are the type of person who has a tough time sticking to any financial constraints, whether a credit card limit or a household budget, it can be extremely tough to put price limits on things as significant as your wedding gown or honeymoon or that two-story lovebirds ice sculpture. Trust me, I get it. I know it's hard to cut out the twice-daily lattes at $3.85 a pop, and it's doubly hard to try to squeeze another week or two between your hair color appointments. But when making a wedding budget and sticking to it, it all comes down to prioritizing. Make a master wedding "wish list" with your fiancé. What elements can you absolutely not go without? What are the elements that make a statement about you as a couple, about your relationship, about your cultural background, and about your values? Put this list in order of importance, down to the things that you'd like to have but would be willing to minimize or eliminate. To be fair, make sure each person gets to make some choices as to what items get top billing. When budget slashes need to be made (which yes, my dear, they most certainly will), begin at the bottom of the list and start chopping. The life lesson in this process (isn't there always a life lesson in every unpleasant experience?) is that you'll eventually realize that you're making judgments about your dreams versus reality. Who wouldn't want Wolfgang Puck in the flesh to cater the wedding of their dreams? But in reality, maybe a Wolfgang-esque menu would be more than fine.

So, talk over your wants and needs with your fiancé, and please, *please* don't knock or insult each other's dreams. You don't have to love his idea of hiring a Metallica cover band as your reception entertainment, but accusing him of being an eighties has-been with bad taste is just plain mean. Nor should your husband-to-be judge you for wanting to borrow your vows from the wedding episode of *Gossip Girl.* Play fair, and think give-and-take. Maybe you believe not having a dinner reception is a deal breaker? Fine, but consider having it on a Sunday night. Rather die than walk down the aisle in anything less that Christian Louboutin on your finicky feet? No problem, but you'll have to cut $500 from the parrot tulip centerpieces. (This is good practice, as my husband and I still play this game every month, right around the time that the pesky folks at American Express send their statement.)

Just like marriage itself, creating your budget is a give-and-take, an exercise in giving significance where it's due and knowing how to slash the spend in the areas that you can easily live without. Yes, it's hard—maybe even excruciatingly so—to stick to your budget when you've been dreaming of your wedding day for a very long time. But be willing to be flexible and look at alternatives to your "dream," and you'll find that you may be able to save big without making too many compromises. The following tips can help you save without skimping and can guide you to a wedding that's possibly even more meaningful than you ever imagined.

Thing 1: No matter how tempting, *never* go into debt to pay for your wedding.

In the recent insecure economic times, I've been continually amazed by couples who have chosen to go into debt in order to pay for a wedding day that's beyond their current means. Starting your new life together as a couple should truly feel like a new beginning—even if you've been dating a long time or even living together before the marriage. That new beginning should come with a built-in sense of excitement and possibility. Sadly, the energy of your new journey together can be dampened by the pressures of starting at less than zero, financially speaking. Just think how you'll feel when those ballooning credit card bills arrive in the mail month after month, when you would rather be putting money aside for your first house, a new business, or any other long-term investment that has real life-changing potential. Without question, your wedding is an incredibly momentous occasion and deserves the best that you can possibly put into it. But think of the peace of mind you'll have if you can be clever enough, creative enough, and realistic enough to make the most of what you can afford to spend on your wedding. Just think twice before you jump into any expenses that will put you into debt and quite likely keep you up at night. Seriously, no one wants to still be paying off their wedding when their own daughter walks down the aisle. That's just depressing.

Thing 2: Get your budget on paper—all of it.

First things first: get your wedding budget down on paper with your fiancé, your families, and anyone else who is chipping in and who will, in turn, expect to have a say in what you spend the money on. If you're fortunate enough to have parents or grandparents willing to contribute to the big day, expect their input. Yes, it's a trade-off.

Sad but true, in every family, weddings are loaded with the potential for overspending, miscommunication, hurt feelings, and a varying degree of family drama. So have the financial discussions as open, honest, and early as possible to get off to the best possible start. Another reason that you should iron out the financial parameters before you get caught up in the adrenaline rush of being a bride is that you'll spare yourself some serious heartache and disappointment by knowing exactly what you can afford to spend on your wedding before you start trying on wedding gowns, booking your favorite band, or even setting the date. Plus, wouldn't it be better to find out now that your future mother-in-law thinks that you waste money like water, rather than later, say while she's making her toast to the two of you at the rehearsal dinner?

Next, stay on track by staying organized. Keep every receipt and contract in a binder, and keep a running tally of what you've spent. Trust me, I've learned this the hard way with my personal budget. Stashing receipts and contracts in a desk drawer here and in a handbag there and shoving them into the glove compartment is a surefire way to lose track of where you stand, and you'll inevitably get into budget trouble in the end.

Force yourself to be detail-oriented to lessen the risk of being taken by surprise when you get your final bills. For every vendor, make sure that in your preliminary budget as well as your quotes and contracts, you've accounted for all of the many incidentals too. You may at first think of these charges as minor, but they add up fast. Don't wind up thousands over budget because you forgot to include sales tax, tips, delivery fees, overtime charges, corkage and cake-cutting fees, and any permits and insurance requirements. Be as specific and exact with the costs as possible.

Finally, to state the obvious, don't go over budget in one area without first finding another area that you can trim by the same amount. Map this out on paper and make sure to be nothing but realistic about how you can even it all out in the end. For example, don't justify going even $100 over budget for wedding favors with the intention of slashing $100 off of the catering budget before you even have a clue of how many guests you'll have.

Thing 3: Discuss your wedding party and preliminary guest list right away; these numbers will dictate much of the expenses.

With your fiancé, decide on your bridesmaids, groomsmen, and anyone else you must include in the wedding party. Keep in mind that the larger the wedding party, the greater the cost, as the number of bouquets, bridemaids gifts, and groomsmen gifts increases. Of course, cutting down on your number of attendants is a way to save some money, but I'm not going to tell you that you can only afford to have two of your five sisters in your wedding! Be realistic about who you truly need and want to have in this significant role on your big day.

Next, compile your guest list, starting with the people you absolutely have to have at your wedding then going down in order of importance to those who may not be quite as vital. Discuss all your "categories" of guests, such as distant relatives, co-workers, children, dates of your single friends, and so on. This preliminary guest count is vital information for moving forward with selecting a venue of the appropriate size, budgeting for your reception, ordering the correct number of invitations, and even getting the necessary number of tables and center-pieces. Be aware that, as mentioned above, parents (or anyone else) who are pitching in toward the wedding costs will most likely expect to have a say in at least part of your guest list. The truth is that unless you actually want family drama surrounding your nuptials, there isn't much you can do about your father's twelve college fraternity brothers and their wives if Daddy is footing the bill for the reception. Though it's tempting to do so, do not underestimate the number of guests that will actually attend. Although it's likely that a certain percentage of your invitees won't attend due to scheduling conflicts, illnesses, or myriad possible reasons, it's dangerous to invite more people than what you can really afford—or will fit into that tiny little Italian restaurant that you have chosen for the reception site. Figuring that an arbitrary percentage of your guest list, say 10 to 20 percent, won't come can get you into a lot of trouble when those "yes" response cards start flooding in. For example, a couple I know recently got married over a major holiday weekend, figuring that many people would decline due to prior family commitments and challenging holiday travel logistics. They were more than a little shocked when nearly everyone on the invite list decided to make the wedding an excuse for a family vacation and were thrilled to come from far and wide!

If the number of people the two of you actually "want" with you when you exchange vows is pretty tiny in relation to the number of other people that you'd feel obligated to have there, now is the time to look at alternative ideas, such as a destination wedding. More on that later.

Thing 4: Make vendors compete for your business.

An upside to the recession is that now more than ever, it's a buyer's market, so wedding vendors have to be quite competitive to gain clients. The cost of the average wedding in the U.S. has steadily climbed over the years, and the wedding industry as a whole seemed protected by an economic bubble—the rare field that was thought to be recession-proof. However, the tide has turned, and for the first time, the average amount of money that a couple has spent on their wedding fell in tandem with the economy (from nearly $28,000 in 2007 to less than $22,000 in 2008 and under $20,000 in 2009, according to *The Wedding Report*), and rest assured that your vendors are hyper-aware of this decline. Even during their busiest times of year, professionals like photographers, caterers, entertainers, and florists are not seeing revenues anywhere near what they enjoyed just a few years ago. The savviest engaged couples are no longer paying premium prices without first doing extensive research and weighing their options. Even the most exclusive wedding venues, those that have historically been booked several years in advance, are seeing some open dates on their calendars. Therefore, your bargaining power is greater than you'd think, and it really pays to shop around. You may even find that your first-choice vendors are willing to price match to get your wedding. So put your game face on and ask, "Is that your best price?" when you get a quote. Sometimes, all you have to do is ask, and you may find a vendor suddenly "remembering" a discounted package or a special incentive that they are offering.

Thing 5: Don't book a consultation with a wedding planner until you know your exact budget.

Without question, a professional wedding planner can be an invaluable asset to any bride and groom. The right planner can give you priceless insight and advice, endless creativity and problem-solving skills, and will have relationships with vendors that can work to your advantage. That being said, hiring a planner is not a necessity, and if your budget is limited, the cost that you'd invest in a wedding planner is probably better spent on the wedding itself. Before I inflame the entire community of wedding planners, let me qualify that opinion. If your wedding is fairly large scale, with upwards of 150 guests, or if you have a highly demanding work schedule that limits the time you can spend on coordinating the event yourself, then a wedding planner can be a smart investment. But if your event is on a relatively manageable scale and money is indeed an object, then the cash you'd spend on a planner's fees are probably better used toward your big line-item expenses like the venue and catering.

If you are considering hiring a professional wedding planner, know that their fees are usually constructed either as a percentage of your overall budget, which can run as high as 15 percent, or a flat fee. Either way, it is, again, important to know exactly what your total budget is before you get into discussions involving a planner's services.

If your budget does allow for you to pay a planner, consider yourself lucky and enjoy that extra peace of mind of having a professional on your side. If you can't afford to pay for full-event coordination, couples with all types of budgets can still consider hiring a coordinator just for the day of the wedding only. Not only is the fee much more reasonable, but it allows the bride and groom to truly enjoy their own wedding rather than be distracted by the many vendors, keep the schedule on time, and handle all of the logistics. Not to mention that if something goes wrong—say the bakery delivers a "Happy Bar

Mitzvah, Eli" cake (hey, it happens) instead of your wedding confection, or your officiant is stuck in traffic—someone else is there to take care of it and keep things running smoothly.

Thing 6: Now is the time to call in favors . . . lots of them.

This should be a no-brainer, but when you're on a budget, be willing to accept help from just about anyone who offers it. Think about the various items that you need. Don't be shy to ask a friend or family member if you can borrow her wedding veil, a fabulous vintage barrette, or a piece of jewelry that you've always admired on them—the old "two birds, one stone" rule applies here, since you'll cover your "something borrowed" requirement while paying a great compliment to the jewelry's owner. Also think of services that you need: Maybe you have a cousin who does calligraphy and would trade her talent for a night of chick flicks and martinis at your apartment? Or a friend who whips up a mean coconut macaroon who would be willing to bake them for the wedding favors? It's even worth looking into the option of having a loved one conduct your ceremony, which means a cheaper but quite poignant wedding. There are laws and religious rules regarding wedding officiants, and they vary by location, but having a loved one become ordained over the Internet has been gaining popularity over the past several years.

In spite of your good intentions and formidable organizational skills, there will inevitably be a number of things that will need to be done at the last minute. Whether the "last minute" means finishing up those D.I.Y. centerpieces the night before the wedding or needing someone to race back to your apartment for your forgotten earrings an hour before your wedding, it's wise to assemble a team of friends or relatives who are reliable, calm under pressure, and preferably not in the wedding. Though your bridesmaids may be happy to help with any last-minute needs, keep in mind that they may be busy with their own last-minute challenges like missing contacts, ripped hems, or hangovers.

If you're truly lucky, you may have quite a talented pool of resources within your own family, so tap into them as much as possible. If someone offers a generic "let me know if you need help with anything," make sure you have a specific request that you can involve them with, from the simplest of tasks such as assembling invitations or favors to more complex assignments like asking to scour the flower mart for you or make sure Grandpa is cut off after his fourth whiskey sour at the reception. If you're afraid of inconveniencing someone, remember that most people don't offer their help if they don't mean it and are, in fact, honored and flattered if you take them up on it.

— 2 —
Otherwise engaged: setting the date

— 2 —
Otherwise engaged: setting the date

Did you know that the length of your engagement could actually be the demise of your well-intentioned budget? Is there an outside factor that is stretching out your engagement time period and wedding date, i.e., you need to wait until after you graduate from medical school, after your fiancé gets back from the Ashram, or after Grandpa gets paroled? Or are you in a rushed situation, maybe because one of you is about to be deployed overseas or is taking your magic show on the road indefinitely? There's no "perfect" engagement length, though most wedding planning advice is based on the tried-and-true twelve-month planning period. Whether yours is longer or shorter than this template, be conscious of the potential budget-busting effects of your timing.

For example, a shorter engagement may help you streamline your plans, keep things simple, and avoid getting wrapped up in the endless extras and extravagant trinkets that brides are constantly bombarded with by the wedding industry. However, you may have limited options for well-priced vendors and locations if everything affordable has already been booked a year in advance. Though it can certainly frazzle your nerves, the great secret of a last-minute wedding is that if you are flexible, it can actually save you money. If your lead time is under two months, you've got a great chance to find fabulous steals if you're up to negotiating. If a venue you're interested in has an open date, chances are they are as eager for your business as you are to secure a site, and the same goes for your cake baker, photographer, and entertainment.

On the flipside, a longer engagement, if done right, can give you more time to save up money, hunt for bargains, negotiate deals, and have a greater selection of available locations and vendors in your price point. But you need willpower because the more time you have to read wedding magazines, go to bridal expos, and ponder every available choice, the more likely you are to be sucked into buying all those tantalizing but completely unnecessary extras (I'm looking at you, custom-made bride and groom bobble heads).

Once you have a rough idea of whether you're looking at a wedding date this calendar year or three years from now, it's time to pick your date. Keeping the following rules in mind can help you stretch your wedding dollars as far as possible.

Thing 7: Be flexible with your date; Saturday evening is not the only choice.

Saturday evening is still the most popular—and most expensive—time to get married. But there are equally elegant yet economical alternatives, such as a Friday evening, Saturday morning or afternoon, or any time on a Sunday. Price out these options and you may be in for a surprise at how much further your money will go. In general, a daytime wedding is less expensive than an evening, and plenty of Sunday afternoon nuptials are just as festive and perfect as their pricier counterparts. And though it's not yet a bona fide trend, there has been a rise in the number of weeknight weddings, particularly the Thursday evening ceremony and cocktail reception.

Thing 8: Like the travel business, weddings also have in-season rates.

In most parts of the country, April to October is prime wedding season and commands the highest prices. Expect to pay premium rates with little bargaining power as well as compete with many other brides for a date. Getting married sometime in November through March can save you 20 to 30 percent for the same event!

Finally, if you dream of a winter wedding, bonus bargain points for you, but note that a holiday wedding, like New Year's Eve or Valentine's Day, is an exception to this rule, with premium prices commanded for banquet spaces and flowers. Additionally, although December is not typically jam-packed with weddings, many event venues do get booked for holiday parties and business events.

— 3 —
Location, location, location

~ 3 ~
Location, location, location

Thing 9: The most economical wedding venue is a multipurpose one, offering beautiful sites for both your ceremony and the reception.

Unless you are absolutely sure that your ceremony will be held in a church or other place of worship, search for a location that can host your entire event. Whether you're practical or just plain lazy, convenience is priceless.

For starters, cutting out the whole headache of coordinating transportation from the ceremony to the reception site for the entire wedding party—not to mention the cost and the potential for traffic delays for you and all your guests—is not an insignificant perk. Plus, you'll pay one site-rental fee instead of two, and you'll maximize multitasking like having

the ceremony chairs moved and later used for dining, moving the ceremony florals to the reception
room, and so on.

**Thing 10: When considering potential wedding
locations, make sure you're comparing apples to
apples.**

What looks like a great deal at first may not be so
great if you'll end up adding loads and loads of
essentials onto it. For example, if the "bring-your-
own" types of venues look like a steal, do your
homework on how much it will cost you to provide
every single item from the catering to the dance
floor. People generally think that putting a crisp
white event tent in a yard or garden is the least
expensive party, until they soon realize that a tent
has to be decorated, air-conditioned or heated, and
outfitted with lighting, flooring, tables, chairs, and
all the other necessities. Take a look at the benefits
of having a virtual one-stop shop for in-house catering, linens, cake, and so on, and even an upscale

hotel can become a better deal than your parents' backyard.

In the same vein, the more naturally beautiful or better dressed a venue is, the more economical it becomes since you'll get away with a far smaller spend on flowers and other embellishments to make it wedding-worthy. Therefore, it's unjust to compare the higher-priced but lavishly appointed antebellum mansion to the bargain-priced banquet hall that will cost a small fortune to dress up.

So, just what makes a great multipurpose wedding location? Here are some of the best.

1. Where to look: hotels. Besides earning posh points, there are practical reasons that hotels are prime wedding locations. Successful hotels are service-oriented and deal with the challenge of housing, entertaining, and feeding several hundred people on a daily basis. Your wedding, no offense, is nothing they haven't seen before from countless weddings, conventions, business conferences, and other events.

The key players, from the reservations manager to the chef to the parking valets, have the whole routine down to a science, and their expertise can save you money and grief in the long run and ensure that you get the experience you've paid for. In most cases, the hotel's catering manager will be your primary contact person, but give a potential location double bonus points if it also includes a wedding coordinator who will oversee every detail of the location's responsibilities from the time you sign the contract to the time your last guest leaves.

Now, before you start envisioning yourself in that golden-gilded grand ballroom, I'm not claiming that booking your city's version of the Plaza is sure to be a steal. But do investigate its rates for weddings, as well as those of your favorite urban retreat, boutique hotel, or even a golf and spa resort, and you may be pleasantly surprised at how far your money will go—and yes, I'm saying this yet again—particularly if you pick a date outside of peak season or on a Friday or Sunday. You might find a fantastic package within your budget, and your out-of-town guests can get a steep discount on swanky rooms.

Finally, if the ballroom is beyond your budget, check out the hotel's restaurant. If it's got a private banquet room and an atmosphere you like, do a price check. Chances are, it's a better deal than the traditional ballrooms that get booked for weddings.

2. Where to look: bed and breakfasts. Loaded with character, B and Bs make fabulous wedding venues, although the largest and best-known ones can cost you nearly the same per person as a top hotel. However, if your wedding will be held in a town that's outside of a trendy resort or vacationing area and off the beaten path as far as tourism goes, a local bed and breakfast retreat could make a truly charming yet cheap venue. There are fantastic finds throughout practically every area of the United States, from old-timey East Coast–style homes dotted amongst antique shops and roadside produce stands, to the cozy farmhouses nested in California's

Wine Country, to the ivy-covered cottages that surround the Great Lakes. Giving your guests a real taste of local flavor not only makes for a unique and memorable trip but gives your wedding a built-in theme as well, whether it's celebrating the turning of the leaves in the fall or the annual strawberry-picking festival or grape-harvesting season. Many bed and breakfast properties feature bucolic gardens ideal for exchanging your vows plus sprawling yards to hold a reception, for a multitasking and picturesque venue that will need little, if any, extra floral decoration. Check out bnbfinder.com for a list of B and Bs that accommodate weddings.

3. Where to look: public places. Nontraditionalists rejoice—here's one for you! Interesting public places in your area, such as the library, zoo, botanical gardens, historical societies, and all types of museums make a unique statement and can be a great deal to boot. The site rental fee—which can be quite pricey when you're talking beach club or country club—is usually quite reasonable for civic hot spots, especially if you're a member. (Take a membership brochure the next time you're at the zoo or the art museum; it's true that membership has its privileges.) This type of site is typically large enough to host a sizable number of guests for the ceremony and reception, plus adds built-in entertainment value too. Well, the library, not so much, but I'm thinking strolls through the zoo or Impressionist exhibits here.

For many couples, the decision will hinge on whether the site has an in-house catering company (which many museums do). If the location you love is an experienced host for fund-raisers, benefits, or membership parties, you'll likely feel more confident with the caliber of catering than if, say, your heart's set on the Museum of Bottle Rockets, and they've never hosted a Boy Scout meeting let alone a wedding. If the caterer is a separate entity, make sure to consider the extra cost and coordination effort of providing outside food, alcohol, wedding cake, and rentals. When possible, try to hire a caterer who has worked with your venue before.

Bargain rental fee aside, sadly, some of these public sites won't be an affordable option in the end, if additional purchases like insurance, security guards, parking attendants, and gorilla wranglers are required. Make sure that your initial price quote contains all of these add-ons before you make cost comparisons between sites.

4. Where to look: your favorite place. Seriously, don't overlook the obvious when searching for your ideal wedding location. Think about the places that make up the settings in your own love story, from the place you met to where he proposed. Maybe it's the chapel at the college you both attended, or the restaurant you went to on your first date and revisit every Valentine's Day, or even your best friend's beach house where you first fell in love—each could be an exceptionally meaningful place to get married. To me, settings that are loaded with character and personality outdo the most extravagant cookie-cutter wedding locations, hands down.

Again, if this sentimental site requires you to provide everything on your own, make sure you've covered every budget line item from biggest (catering, tents) to smallest (heat lamps, champagne glasses) to calculate the total cost.

Thing 11: Sometimes, you can't beat city hall.

Before you scoff at the idea of an intimate (also known as inexpensive) civic ceremony, consider the "new" city hall wedding. Now more than ever, eloping is a very attractive alternative to the lengthy planning period, inevitable stress, and significant cost of a traditional wedding. Though the Las Vegas wedding chapel elopement is a cultural icon in its own right, the travel and hotel costs may be too expensive for your budget. Save on both by staying in your hometown.

A city hall wedding can be as simple or elaborate as you wish. You can go the traditional route by wearing a white dress, carrying a bouquet, and decorating the room with flowers, and even having a best man and maid of honor. Though the number of guests is normally limited to around ten or less (which varies by location), you can still invite as many loved ones as you like to your reception. By minimizing the ceremony cost, just think of how much money you'd have left over to put into a cool reception, the honeymoon, or even a house down payment.

No longer the boring and bureaucratic stand-in-line-and-sign quickie nuptials, some city halls have gotten creative and dramatically upped their game, even putting a dose of chic into the ultra-cheap.

Search the government Web site of your own city, big cities within driving distance, or any town that simply strikes your fancy for details on their facilities, marriage license requirements, and fees. True, most city halls are seriously lacking in the glamour quotient, but you may be pleasantly surprised to find a more progressive one in your area. The cities with the most bridal-buzzworthy civic services are New

York, with its newly renovated Office of the County Clerk located in Manhattan (see cityclerk.nyc.gov), complete with a flower shop and modern-style chapels; San Francisco, which features ceremonies in your choice of a private room or the City Hall Rotunda and even offers a full two-hour reception package for up to 200 people (see sfgov.org) at a reasonable rental fee; and, of course, Las Vegas (see AccessClarkCounty.com).

Thing 12: A destination wedding may cost less than a small traditional wedding at home.

Does your wedding vision lean toward the intimate, personal, and informal realm? Does the honeymoon seem more important to you than the actual wedding? Does the thought of being surrounded by a hundred or more guests give you a full-on panic attack? If so, then you are hardly alone—destination weddings are an incredibly fast-growing phenomenon and a trend that isn't going to wane any time soon. I believe the destination wedding is my generation's alternative to elopement. An ingenious alternative, I might add, since a destination wedding is a shame-free way to be utterly selfish and shockingly affordable.

By being selfish but free of negative connotations, the bride and groom can do the often-impossible feat of limiting the number of guests to just those they cannot live without. This is done in one of two ways: either by declaring the wedding to be "intimate" and inviting only family and the closest friends, hoping that all of your extraneous relatives and random acquaintances will get the drift of "intimate" and not expect an invitation; or by inviting everyone under the sun while knowing that the combination of travel logistics and cost will keep a great percentage of your invite list at home. Destination weddings, by virtue, usually end up being on a smaller, less formal, more manageable scale than traditional ones—unless most of your nearest and dearest own private jets or you're paying for everyone's airfares (in which case, why are you reading this book?)—allowing your money to go further.

Whether you want to keep your guest count down, it is only fair to give your guests as much advance notice as possible, particularly if your wedding date falls near a holiday or other busy travel time, or if passports are required. As with all weddings, know the peak season for the location you're considering. Although you may not want to get married during the official off-season (hurricanes don't care that it's your wedding day), choosing a date at the very end of it could be a great way to get a major discount without major risks. Even during the busy season, most resorts consider Sunday through Thursday to be slower days and offer discounts for events that take place during that time frame.

Resorts and hotels in popular wedding destinations seriously streamline the whole wedding planning process. They provide all-inclusive packages for just about every budget, and most offer deep discounts if you stay there the rest of the week for your honeymoon. Many couples end up with a much longer trip than what they thought they could afford, certainly a happy way to start off a marriage.

If you're not a control freak and can handle the thought of working with vendors without meeting with them personally, you'll want to award extra-credit points to resorts that include a wedding coordinator as part of the package. An on-site coordinator will have experience and relationships with the local vendors, which means that a great deal of the planning stress will fall on her instead of you. Under your direction, the coordinator will be the one juggling the many vendors and keeping everything on schedule while you're at home, living your life. Sounds like a sweet deal, huh?

Though it is indeed counterintuitive, traveling to a lush, exotic locale to share your wedding day with the people you love most can cost less than a simple wedding at home and a no-frills honeymoon. All without using that pesky "elope" word.

Thing 13: Your wedding dollar goes furthest in

Las Vegas.

As much as other popular wedding destinations try to compete with Las Vegas for the most bang for the buck, none of them come close. Whether you plan to elope with just the two of you and spend a couple hundred bucks, or celebrate with dozens of your nearest and dearest for several thousand dollars, your money will go further in Vegas than in any other major U.S. city. In fact, tying the knot in even the most upscale casino hotel chapel complete with a limo, flowers, photographer, wedding cake, and a reception can cost you up to 50 to 75 percent less than a comparable wedding elsewhere in the country! For example, a typical, "traditional" wedding and dinner reception that would cost $20,000 in Los Angeles can be very closely matched in Vegas for as little as $10,000 at a Vegas hotel for the same number of guests.

Weddings are big revenue in Vegas—next to gambling, of course—and the advantage of having so many independent wedding chapels and hotel and casino chapels is that the competition for your business makes the good deals even greater. Particularly during "off" times, such as weekdays and non-holiday weeks, brides have bargaining power that can translate to group discounts for airfare and hotel rooms, wedding package discounts, and other incentives like restaurant, spa, and shopping credits, and even gambling money.

The Vegas wedding image has long suffered from the cliché of ultra-cheesy, quickie nuptials performed by an Elvis impersonator in a tragically tacky wedding chapel. But now there are actually countless alternatives to suit your own style, from simple and elegant to glamorous to just plain outrageous. The top-tier hotels, such as the Venetian and Bellagio, have beautifully appointed wedding chapels and relationships with vendors that rival the style and taste level of any other metropolitan area, for a modern, sophisticated event that is a far cry from the old "running-off-to-Vegas" images. Like other destination weddings, Vegas events are planned and priced as packages, and there is a package to fit virtually every budget. Events range from a simple ceremony for just the two of you, including the marriage license, starting at under $200, to a formal dinner reception at one of the myriad upscale restaurants for ten, twenty, or even a hundred guests.

— 4 —

Your wedding style: it can look luxe for less

– 4 –

Your wedding style: it can look luxe for less

Unlike the weddings of our parents' generation, it seems like basically anything goes when it comes to styles and themes of today's weddings. The options are limited only by your creativity, from a timeless, all-white wedding, to a black-and-silver Art Deco supper club theme, to a sunset fiesta theme swathed in shades of orange and hot pink. Though interesting, your style can be good news and bad news because brides can feel pressured to create nothing short of spectacular with their wedding style, which may seem impossible if you're on a budget. However, no matter what your budget is, there are plenty of ways to make a stylish statement that reflects your personality. Do some brainstorming on colors and decorating ideas that speak to you, and use resources besides wedding magazines and Web sites. Inspiration can come from anywhere, but some of the most unique ideas can be borrowed from movies, interior design magazines, fabric stores, restaurants, and even flea markets. Once you've decided on your unifying theme or color story, use it to organize your thoughts and ideas and keep your overall look cohesive. Also use it as an editing tool to keep your planning and budget on track by asking yourself if something you think is a must-have really fits in with your overall concept. If not, move on. Though an open mind and unlimited imagination are your best assets, there are some wedding styles that are innately challenging to produce without unlimited funds. Following are some hints for finding the balance between awe-inspiring and affordable.

Thing 14: Overdoing it on decor can cost you your budget—and your sanity.

The simplest way to streamline the cost of reception decor is to choose a venue that has already done much of the work for you. What this means is if you need to transform a sleek, modern, gallery-like space into a frilly Victorian parlor look, then good luck. Whether or not you're stuck on a certain theme when you look at potential sites, do try to see the room when it's set up for an event. Imagine how your color scheme or style will translate when it's played out in that room. Ask yourself if you can easily create your vision without having to spend a lot of money. Will you be able to convey your style with simple (and inexpensive) touches like clusters of pillar candles or colorful table runners, or will you need to bring in a truckload of palm trees and exotic birds to get your message across? Without spending five figures on flowers, brides with even the most limited budgets can make the most boring space feel fabulously festive by hanging up teeny twinkle lights, Chinese lanterns, or giant paper flowers. And, I've said it before, but it's worth repeating: the more natural or built-in beauty that a wedding venue offers, whether it's from abundant flowers and blossoming trees, stunning architecture, or a simply breathtaking view, the less you'll have to spend on flourishing it.

Thing 15: A modern, minimalist wedding is the cheapest to create without looking cheap.

The typical bride can so easily get carried away with elaborate, ultra-romantic wedding themes, like autumn in Tuscany, French Provincial, Alice in Wonderland, and other complex decor ideas that are real budget busters. Like an epic period film, these visions require countless intricate details in order to get it just right.

On the flipside, just think of how much less cash it would take to produce the most sophisticated, urban-chic wedding with very few accessories. The beauty of ultra-modern decor is that it looks like a strong style statement rather than a budget statement. Now more than ever, the economy is making simplicity more in vogue than extravagance, so going minimalist is one trend that actually works in your favor. You can easily make an utterly elegant statement with an all-white color story, or make white pop with a single accent color like silver, grass-green, espresso brown, or even coral. Use the uber-chic minimalist atmosphere of many a big-city restaurant as your inspiration. Think simple tablescapes of an orchid bloom floating in a clear round bowl or a single floral stem in a bud vase. Better yet, alternate the centerpieces on the tables, so that some have florals, some are adorned with clusters of pillar candles in various widths and heights surrounded by Spanish moss, while others are accented with smooth mahogany or teak wooden bowls filled with pears. Set amidst crisp white linens, even decor as economical as this looks like a million bucks. Not to mention the best part: your guests will be so enthralled by your striking yet understated Zen-ness that they'll never guess it didn't cost a fortune.

Thing 16: Choosing a unique color scheme can be

more difficult—and more expensive—to pull off than more popular ones.

I'm not saying that you have to go with a black-and-white color scheme if you're on a budget, but it is definitely an accessible way to create an elegant look without costing a bundle. Because it's a color combo found in all types of events from birthday parties to Bar Mitzvahs, the accoutrements are easy to find in any price point, from party supply stores to craft stores and home goods retailers, all places where you're not stuck having to pay wedding prices for simple white milk glass vases or basic black grosgrain ribbon.

Color combinations on the more creative side of the spectrum, like apple green with pink or chocolate brown with pale blue, are recent trends that make for a spectacular vision, but take some finesse to get just right. The truth is that trying to make these sophisticated combos work on the cheap can end up looking, well, sadly cheap. For example, the right pale blue can look chic and subtle while the wrong one can look better suited for a cheesy baby shower. So if you're considering a more modern color story, you must think about how it will translate from every aspect from your florals to your bridesmaids dresses. To be blunt, envision all six of your twenty- or thirty-something bridesmaids, in their various shapes and hair colors, in that chartreuse taffeta you think you love, and ask yourself if that looks as fantastic on them as it does on the swatch card.

The same challenges apply for an eclectic palette, like peacock blue with cherry red and metallic gold. Festive, yes, but difficult to get just right on a budget, because you'll need more complex centerpieces and room decor to pull the look together in a beautiful, connected way. Skimp on the florals and accessories, and you'll risk ending up with a reception room that looks disjointed or downright confusing. Whatever colors you go with, save your sanity by thinking color family rather than exact match. If you are dead set on finding tablecloths and votive candles that match the exact shade of your fuchsia cymbidium orchids, well, good luck to you. You'll run into many a headache, custom-order fees, and probably late-night anxiety attacks. Don't say I didn't warn you. Realize that using the main shade as inspiration for a range of similar shades can be much more economical, look just as well-planned, and quite likely end up looking even more stunning than the painstaking matchy-matchy look.

— 5 —
The reception (or, Why rubber chicken eats up your budget)

– 5 –

The reception (or, Why rubber chicken eats up your budget)

It's true: even the most unpretentious wedding reception will devour an average of thirty-five to fifty percent of a couple's budget. Considering that it's your most significant spend, it's crucial to know what you can trim while still giving your guests a fun and memorable experience.

The type of meal you serve your guests, and how it's served, largely determines where your catering budget will start. Many caterers have a fixed per-person starting price, the highest being for a sit-down dinner, and decreasing with a family-style seated dinner, buffet-style dinner, and luncheons. This is just a starting point; the final price will, of course, depend on the specific foods you choose.

So how can you be a frugalista foodie without skimping on the reception?

Thing 17: Lower your food costs by serving a buffet-style dinner, a luncheon or brunch, or even a cocktail-and-hors d'oeuvres reception.

True, buffets did once have a bad rap for being quantity-over-quality spreads of lukewarm, mediocre dishes like bland pastas and rubbery chicken. But that is no longer the case now that buffets have evolved into food stations and taken on a whole new meaning. Today's typical buffets offer something for everyone, including traditional carving stations of roast beef and turkey alongside creative fusion-cuisine, gourmet pizza bars, and even sushi chefs. A great lunch buffet of exquisite salads, antipasto, and seafood trumps the outdated wedding staples like Chicken Kiev, hands down.

That being said, don't assume that a buffet is automatically more cost-effective than a sit-down meal. The cost per person will hinge upon your food choices and the size of the staff required for it. Work with your caterer to find the best menu choices for your price point.

The beauty of a lunch reception is that for the same food, the price per person is significantly less than for a dinner—typically 20 to 30 percent less, not to mention that your guests are likely to drink less at that time of day as well.

If a full meal just isn't in your budget, there's no rule that your reception has to be held at a mealtime. Include a phrase like "Cocktail Reception to Follow" below the ceremony information on your invitation so that guests don't show up starving, expecting to be served a heavy lunch or dinner. Instead, entertain guests with a post-ceremony cocktail hour with passed appetizers that look and feel festive while giving everyone a chance to mingle. With a little booze, a little food, and a slice of wedding cake, everyone feels like they've celebrated the happy couple, and you haven't blown your nest egg on rubber chicken, right?

Keep in mind that cocktail receptions are typically held between 5 and 7 P.M., which may be a problem for a Friday evening event. On any workday, make sure you give your guests enough time to deal with rush-hour traffic so they don't miss all the fun.

The daytime version of the cocktail reception is the champagne-and-cake reception, which is kicked up a notch with luscious desserts and signature cocktails as well. The best time frame for this type of party is between 3 and 5 P.M., to avoid overlapping either lunchtime or dinnertime.

If you feel that a cocktail party isn't quite enough, price out a morning wedding and brunch reception. Not only will it earn you bonus points for uniqueness, it's by far the best deal—and besides, who doesn't love going out to Sunday brunch? No matter the size of your guest list, getting married early in the day has some great advantages and could be the key to making your vision fit within your budget. For one thing, a late-morning or early afternoon reception is typically shorter than the evening party-til-they-kick-us-out receptions, cutting down on the staffing hours for the caterer, the number of hours for your photographer, videographer, and band or DJ, as well as on alcohol consumption.

Also, brunch fare is lighter and less expensive than lunch or dinner but doesn't have to feel less special. Think brunch buffet stations with made-to-order om-elettes, crepes, French toast, and waffles, plus lav-ish displays of fresh fruit, pastries, bagels and lox, and more. Set up teacarts with loads of herbal teas, coffees, and fresh juices along with Bloody Marys, mimosas, and chilled white wine, and you can still have an elegant reception for a fraction of the price of a dinner at the same venue—sometimes as much as half the cost.

Thing 18: If you're set on using pricey ingredients, use them wisely.

If you are a true culinary connoisseur and absolutely must serve an ultra-expensive item because it's your favorite food, be smart about how you use it. For example, you and your spouse-to-be live on Italian white truffles and can't imagine a celebration without them? Fine, incorporate them into the hors d'oeuvres, use them in a sauce, or serve an entrée duo consisting of a small portion of these deal-breaker truffles alongside a portion of chicken or steak. Very elaborate appetizers can certainly be followed with equally impressive yet reasonably priced meals, built around interesting seasonal dishes. A great combination would be a soup course, such as pumpkin or gazpacho, followed by an entrée of spinach- and ricotta-filled pasta with vegetable tartlets, or a simple but succulent roasted chicken with delicious crispy potatoes au gratin or root vegetables, or other dishes that are special, colorful, and flavorful without incorporating expensive ingredients. And keep in mind that most people prefer these beautiful bargainista dishes over more expensive dishes like steak, lamb, or veal anyway!

The truth is, no matter how painstaking you are about choosing the most interesting, gourmet-inspired dishes, your wedding reception is not a five-star restaurant. Catering comes down to preparing a large quantity of food for a large number of people, and keeping it heated in the kitchen or on chafing dishes. Thus, the chance of your amazing-sounding dish tasting as fantastic as it does when made to order at your favorite five-star restaurant is slim to none. And that's really okay, because no sane person attends a wedding with the hope or expectation of dining on the greatest meal of his life.

Thing 19: When it comes to catering, the devil is in the details.

What may seem like details and the dreaded "miscellaneous" charges can really add up and quickly turn that affordable catering quote into a budget buster. When reviewing catering quotes, make sure that what you think is the final cost actually is the final cost.

Whether you're looking at a total figure or a price per person, ask about any additional costs and get them specifically in writing on your contract. Details like sales tax, gratuities for wait staff, overtime charges, and applicable corkage fees and cake-cutting fees must be accounted for in your catering budget so there are no nasty surprises when you're handed the bill. If your event is at a hotel or other venue that requires valet parking, negotiate a per-car parking rate (including a tip for the attendant) and have that included in your package. Never expect guests to pay for valet parking when attending your wedding. Yes, it's another expense on your ever-growing cost sheet, but it's part of being a gracious host to your guests. Like so many other details, consider it the cost of doing business when you choose a hotel wedding.

Thing 20: This isn't Delta; there's no such thing as a free upgrade.

Upgrades are the wedding equivalent of the "extras" that a car salesman will talk you into—and they will cost you. What I really want to tell you is to never,

ever fall for the upgrades. But I know you won't listen and you'll want to just "take a peek" at the Muted Ochre Tablecloths . . . and then the Antique Brocade Chair Covers . . . and next thing you know, you've fallen for the Platinum Dinner Plate Charger . . . and that's how you go over your budget.

If you're feeling low and think your budget is keeping you from adding enough color or decoration to your reception, be creative. For example, if ordering white or gold banquet chairs is too expensive, go with the regular chairs but instead of paying for chair covers, you could tie inexpensive sashes or ribbon around the backs of the chairs, or add splashes of color to the tablecloths by scattering flower petals on them. Remember, even the most plain reception room will look more colorful and lively once it's embellished with your centerpieces and other florals. If you fall in love with the idea of adding colorful accents, make the most impact by ordering organza overlays for the tables along with colored napkins, but scale back on the centerpieces by the same amount of money.

Even the tables themselves are up for discussion when it comes to your budget. Though tradition usually dictates large, round banquet tables for ten to twelve people, event-planning trends can get you off track. For example, in some cities, smaller, square, eight-person tables are all the rage, and in other places it's long rectangular tables, both of which can cost a bit more. From a price perspective, going with larger tables, whether square or round, that seat ten to twelve guests, is the best way to minimize the rental costs of the tables and tablecloths, and even the centerpieces, since you won't need as many.

My point is, it's dangerously easy to get talked into things you don't need and never even knew existed, so don't jump into anything. Don't ever agree to an upgrade without first asking for the exact cost, and even then just think it over for a day or two before you commit to it. Chances are, once you've weighed that additional (superfluous) cost against the necessities you've got to pay for (like the marriage license and an officiant), you'll realize that the round tables and standard white linens look just fine.

Thing 21: Don't get soaked by the cost of alcohol.

Alcohol can be a real blow to your wedding budget, and estimating the total cost is not easy. Standard rules like 2.5 drinks per guest aren't always helpful since the time of day, type of drinks you serve, average age of your guests, and length of your reception all play a role in the overall consumption.
That being said, there are ways to control your alcohol costs without resorting to a cash bar (please, just don't do it; don't). The simplest way to manage the booze budget is by limiting your guests' options. Serving only wine and beer is a great solution that will usually be fine with most guests. Beware that while serving wine and beer only is smart, it certainly won't do you any good in the end if you select pricey wines. Taste test several wines that are $10 or

less per bottle before you consider pricier options—you may be pleasantly surprised.

A fabulous yet frugal trend is adding a signature drink to the beer-and-wine-only bar. A signature cocktail can add a festive and personal touch to your reception and doesn't have to increase your alcohol budget at all. Ask your caterer for a large glass dispenser for the bar (or, better yet, snatch one up at a second-hand store) and make it into a stunning showpiece by filling it with any type of colorful signature drink—a fruit-filled sangria, a sunny limoncello dotted with lemon and lime slices, a mango-and-vanilla-bean infused vodka—anything that makes an enticing statement to your guests.

If you do choose to serve a full bar, you can still trim costs by offering only one house brand of each type of liquor (which you've chosen by price, of course) rather than three top-shelf whiskey brands, four spendy vodkas, five brands of scotch, and so on. In most mixed drinks, it's difficult for all but the most finicky drinker to notice the difference in taste. Another smart save is to restrict the open bar to just the hours before and after the lunch or dinner, serving only wine and nonalcoholic drinks during the meal. Champagne costs more than any other type of alcohol, so be smart about how you serve it. Consider limiting it to just the traditional champagne toast, either at the start of the dinner or during the cake cutting. While the amount served for a toast is a far cry from the cash drain of keeping the champagne flowing freely all party long, it's still a significant cost. To cut the price, consider serving a nice sparkling white wine, such as Cava varieties from Spain or Californian champagnes, with myriad choices well under $20 per bottle, or even a champagne cocktail like a Kir Royale or Bellini. Or, buck tradition and forgo the champagne spend altogether, and your guests will simply toast with whatever they are already drinking.

Finally, know your options for how you are charged for alcohol. Most venues offer a choice of either a consumption-based charge, which means that you are only charged for what your guests drink, or an open-bar charge of a per-guest flat fee. (Obviously, if you've got a crowd of very light drinkers, go with the consumption bar.) Or, if your location requires that you pre-order all of the alcohol from them, it can't hurt to ask if they offer "buy back" on any unopened bottles so that you haven't wasted loads of money if you overpurchased. Better yet is a venue that allows you to bring in your own alcohol, so that you can purchase it on your own from a store that has a buy-back policy.

Thing 22: Cake costs are largely determined by the labor involved.

The cost of the wedding cake is more than just the ingredients—it's also determined by the labor, the size, and the height. Even the most basic white cake–buttercream-frosting creation can skyrocket in price if it's six tiers high and painstakingly covered in miniscule hand-rolled fondant roses.
When you're looking at all of the architecturally

extraordinary cakes in wedding magazines, remember that the more elaborate it is, the more you'll pay. The flavors you choose, the number of tiers, plus the amount of time your baker spends making, assembling, and decorating it all add up. Intricate sugar or fondant flowers, which are handcrafted, cost far more than having your baker flourish the cake with fresh edible flowers, fruit, or a simple icing design. There are many inexpensive ways you can beautifully embellish your cake, whether it's with sugared fruits and berries for an autumnal wedding, or white edible orchids on a simple, Zen-chic cake, or even figs and champagne grapes adorning a chocolate-frosted cake at a vineyard wedding. Some of the most charming and striking cakes I've seen have actually been the least expensive, with simple, easy-to-do flourishes like white frosting polka dots or a blanket of white coconut flakes atop plain frosting and topped off with a cute cluster of fresh daisies, orange and lemon slices, or a bright tropical flower. Regarding ingredients, though hiring an organic baker is certainly noble, be prepared to pay a premium for all of that wholesome goodness. The same goes for any dietary restrictions, like needing a cake to be gluten-free or vegan. When made in such a large amount, a cake with special ingredients will run considerably more than the going rate of three to five dollars per slice. Additionally, upgrading from the good old-fashioned wedding cake flavors like vanilla, strawberry, lemon, and coconut to trendy concoctions like passion fruit, green tea, or Grand Marnier will add to the cost as well.

You may think it's crucial to match the cake frosting color to your wedding colors, but note that certain colors of icing, particularly those that veer from the traditional pastels like pink and green, may have an additional cost. Buttercream frosting, which tastes better and is easier to work with than fondant, is also the cheaper of the two.

Surprisingly, even the shape makes a difference.

Square cakes look modern and unique but can cost more than the traditional round tiers. It takes longer to even out all of those square edges and frost than a round cake, and some bakers take that into account. Finally, it's easy to fall in love with one of the incredible cake toppers now available—from custom-made miniature versions of the bride and groom to super-cute and kitschy vintage couples, or even ultra-expensive porcelain, china, or ceramic creations. But before you fork over that credit card, check with your mom or grandmother to see if she's still got her own wedding cake topper hidden away somewhere. You just might uncover the perfect accompaniment to your cake—with a cost of zero and extra credit for serving as your "something borrowed."

Thing 23: Go with your venue's baker for the best wedding cake deal.

Your wedding site will prefer that you go with their baker (or their in-house pastry chef) and will charge an extra cake-cutting fee, up to a few dollars per person, if you go with an outside vendor. If your heart is set on a specific baker, total the cake-cutting fees along with the bakery's delivery charge and assembly charge, and make sure that the extra cost is really worth it to you.

Thing 24: You really need only one real cake tier for your cake cutting.

There are several brilliant ways to dramatically cut down on the size and cost of your wedding cake without your guests knowing the difference. Many couples order one small but intricately decorated cake to use for the cake cutting but serve the guests cupcakes, which are not only adorable and trendy but never require a cake-cutting fee. For a little more money, you can upgrade those cupcakes to Lilliputian-sized individual wedding cakes for the guests, a dessert surprise that garners the kind of "oohs and aahs" and declarations of extraordinary cuteness normally awarded only to puppies and babies. What could be better than amusing your guests with something so hip and unexpected while ditching that pesky cake-cutting fee and $9-per-slice traditional wedding cake?

If you prefer the look of a larger, multi-tiered cake but don't want the major spend, you can get really clever and ask the baker to make dummy layers out of frosting-enrobed Styrofoam for everything but the tier that you'll cut into. Your guests are served slices from a less-expensive sheet cake that's hidden away in the kitchen, and no one is the wiser, as long as the icing matches the couple's cake.

If an ornate, frosting-swathed cake just isn't your thing, you can even forgo the traditional wedding cake altogether and display a table with a dozen of your favorite desserts, or order a tower of decorated cupcakes, cookies, or even bite-sized cheesecakes. It will still look charming in your photos, you can still feed each other that customary first bite of the treat you choose, and you'll have quite a fancy spread of confections for your guests for less than the price of a cake.

Finally, I'm in love with this truly inventive idea that slashes the cost of both your wedding cake and your flowers: the bride and groom have a mini, two-person sized cake for their cutting, while every reception table is appointed with its own wedding cake that serves the guests at that table and serves as a whimsical centerpiece. (Well, at least until it's devoured, so push your cake cutting to the reception's end!) Not only is it an ingenious twist on the wedding cake tradition, but it gives the whole ceremonial cake cutting a very fun, interactive spirit as each table cuts into their cake just after the bride and groom cut into theirs.

— 6 —

Entertainment: it can make or break your party

— 6 —

Entertainment: it can make or break your party

I can't ignore the trend of budget-conscious couples plugging an iPod into a sound system and hoping for a fantastic reception . . . but I strongly advise against it. Getting people up on the dance floor—people of a wide variety of ages and tastes, no less—takes some real skill, and you get what you pay for. A great DJ or the leader of a band can act as master of ceremonies, "read" the crowd to choose the best crowd-pleasing music from different eras, and keep the momentum going with a smart mix of slow-paced and fast-paced songs, including love songs, dance grooves, and the wedding reception clichés like YMCA and—God help us—the chicken dance. Particularly if you're planning an evening reception, where the dancing can go on for several hours, you're looking at a substantial expense, but there are ways to keep it in check.

Thing 25: Hiring a DJ is typically far less costly than hiring a band.

It's easy to see why over 80 percent of couples are choosing DJs over live bands for their reception entertainment: in most cities, the cost of a DJ starts as low as $100 per hour, while the average cost for a five-piece band for a four-hour reception is several thousand dollars. If you're lucky enough to have a friend who is a fabulous amateur DJ at parties, then by all means do consider hiring him for your reception. Just make sure that you provide the playlist, a specific "don't-play" list, and any other instructions so that you're not taken by surprise when he chooses to blare "Brick House" for the father-daughter dance. And though it may seem obvious to you, a DJ may not automatically switch from blaring dance music to conversation-friendly, lower-energy background music during the meal service unless you instruct him to do so.

Thing 26: If you hire a band for your reception music, try to make it multipurpose.

Find out if you can hire a few of the band members to play the music for your ceremony and during cocktails. Extending the working hours of a few musicians could cost you less than hiring separate musicians, such as a string quartet, for the ceremony or cocktail hour.

Thing 27: The best wedding bands are not always wedding bands.

In the same way that putting the word "wedding" in front of any item automatically raises the price, the rates charged by bands marketed as wedding entertainment are typically significantly higher than the price of local bands that play at restaurants, bars, or community events. Plenty of these bands are hugely talented, can play a variety of music, and know how to keep a crowd engaged and energized without commanding that "wedding" premium price. It's absolutely worth your time to spend a few weekend evenings visiting restaurants and clubs that have live entertainment to see if you discover the perfect musicians for your reception, whether it's a swing band, a salsa group, a Beatles cover band, a female vocalist, or even a kitschy lounge singer. The wedding receptions that stand out most in my mind had entertainment that was a little offbeat and a lot of fun.

Thing 28: An iPod with a great playlist can stand in for cocktail music.

Though, as previously stated, your reception will fare better with the personality and energy of a live person to keep things hopping, there's no reason why you have to shell out for live entertainment during the cocktail hour. This is the time to put that iPod to use as ambiance music to fill the gap between the ceremony and the reception.

— 7 —
Frugalista florals:
snobbery will get you nowhere

— 7 —
Frugalista florals: snobbery will get you nowhere

From the bouquets carried by the bride and brides-maids, to floral arrangements that flourish the altar or make up a chuppah, to the floral centerpieces on your reception tables, flowers play a significant role in a wedding. Not surprising, the cost can be significant as well, with most couples allocating up to 10 percent of their wedding budget to flowers. The average bride has no clue just how expensive flowers can be, and usually starts off with grandiose plans of pumpkin-sized bouquets, chandeliers dripping with Black Magic roses, and an aisle runner blanketed in ankle-deep peonies. Then she meets with a florist, and once she has recovered from the initial sticker-shock, she must find a way to create a lush look without the lavish bill. It can be done.

First, regardless of the type of flowers you choose, realize that as with wedding cakes, the hidden cost is in the labor. Therefore, cascades and other complex arrangements that require wiring and lots of time to create cost more than simple centerpieces or hand-tied bouquets. Just one more reason why simple is usually best. Here are other ways to get a grip on your flower funds.

Thing 29: Put your floral budget where it shows.

When your spending power is limited, you've got to put your dollars where they make the most visual impact. It's largely a personal choice: some brides feel that bouquets show the most in the wedding photos that will be looked at forever and choose to invest more cash there than on centerpieces, while other brides can't imagine a reception room with anything less than ornate towers of flowers on every table.

Another way to allocate your floral spend is to consider that if your ceremony will be only half an hour long, place that budget at a minimum and splurge on the arrangements that will be enjoyed for many hours during your reception. For a ceremony in a church or other large area that needs bigger flowers just to be noticed, choose large-headed flowers like hydrangea, cabbage roses, or football mums so that you can fill up space without buying as many. (And, of course, do multitask these arrangements by using them to flourish the entrance of the reception room, on the stage or cake table, or anywhere else that could use a dose of color.)

If the rows of chairs or pews look plain or severe without any embellishment, look for cheaper alternatives to the ornate floral swags typically used. A visit to any craft store can yield quite an array of ridiculously easy—and cheap—ideas befit for even the clumsiest of crafters. Chains like Michaels are the holy grail of artificial flowers, with departments deeply stocked with just about every color and variety you can imagine, as well as a head-spinning selection of ribbon, accoutrements like fake butterflies and birds, and all types of wires and adhesives. Depending on the style or theme of your event, you could flourish the back of each chair or even just the end-of-aisle chairs by wrapping a silk flower "lei" or flower chain, or even a length of satin or gros-grain ribbon tied in a bow. Similarly, a small basket filled with flower petals and tied with ribbon, or a tight bunch of lavender or baby's breath wrapped with raffia could decorate the end of each pew in a church. In the end, remember that once your ceremony starts, all eyes will be on you and your groom, not on the chairs.

If you'll be exchanging vows beneath a chuppah in a Jewish wedding ceremony, you'll likely be shocked at the wide range of prices florists charge to create or rent this type of canopy for you. A chuppah can cost anywhere from a hundred dollars to well into the thousands, depending on just how elaborately its decorated. It's easy to be taken in by a photo of a grandiose chuppah, adorned with chandeliers and dripping with cascades of roses, lilies, and peonies, but ask your florist how he or she can scale it back to fit your budget. A more natural or rustic chuppah constructed of branches entwined with ivy, greenery, and a few roses can look just as magical as an outrageously over-the-top one, and your guests will still be enthralled by the simple romance of it all.

Thing 30: Be brutally realistic about your abilities before you decide to do the flowers yourself.

Beware the allure of DIY (do-it-yourself) when it comes to your wedding flowers. The multitude of how-to books and television shows on floral design make it look so simple, don't they? But as with anything else that takes any degree of skill and practice—for example, sewing your own wedding gown or building your own house—be honest about what you can really accomplish, what you have time for, and whether the potential savings is worth the potential drama. For example, if your craft capabilities top out at tying a ribbon around a bottle of wine, think twice about constructing complicated, wired floral cascades on your own. It won't be a pretty sight. Ditto if your patience is limited, if you're prone to leave things until the last minute (as in an hour before your wedding guests arrive), or if you crack under pressure.

That being said, if you envision simple arrangements and hand-tied (or clutch) bouquets made of sturdy, user-friendly flowers (not fragile blooms like orchids or gardenias) and have a backup team of family and friends that can pitch in last-minute if you're struck by a petal-induced panic attack, then you're a good candidate for DIY. A great place to start is to scout out the costs of your preferred flowers at a local farmer's market, an online florist such as wholeblossoms.com, or even retailers like Costco, Home Depot, Whole Foods, and Trader Joe's. No matter what, don't assume that by choosing a so-called common flower, like roses or daisies, that you can simply show up at your local flower mart or supermarket the morning of your wedding and find exactly what you need in the right quantity and in full-bloom. (Do your homework on which floral varieties bloom over a period of days before they become fully opened.)

Thing 31: Think outside the (flower) box for unique, cost-effective decorations.

One upside to a lethargic economy is that it forces brides to become more creative and open-minded. There's no point to being a snob when it comes to flowers, so don't ignore a certain breed just because it's not typically used for weddings. For example, people don't always associate mums, carnations, hydrangea, or daisies with weddings as much as they do roses, calla lilies, and peonies, but these less-pricey picks can be just as colorful and stunning whether used alone or mixed with other blooms. Hydrangeas, as well as other large-headed flowers, are especially smart buys because they take up space, so you'll need less of them to make an impact.
For real savings on decor, think of ways to incorporate nonfloral elements, including feathers; fruits such as pomegranates, pears, lemons, limes, and

champagne grapes; vegetables such as artichokes, squash, gourds, and even Indian corn for an autumnal fête; and natural elements such as branches, pinecones, and seashells into your centerpieces and even your bouquets.

Don't underestimate the ambiance power of candles, which are, pardon the pun, burning hotter than ever and a seriously recession-friendly touch. Think rows of hanging lanterns for illuminating an outdoor reception, including walkways. Adding tall, tapered candles to any flower centerpiece gives it more drama and height for next to nothing. Flickering votives or tea lights add an ethereal feel to any room, and are especially beautiful when placed alongside a floral centerpiece. A clear glass hurricane candle encircled by flower petals is simple and chic, and pillar candles in varying heights and widths create interest when clustered together or interspersed with flowers. The point is, the less your arrangements rely on flowers, the more affordable (and interesting) they become. Consider how striking a few peacock plumes would look in an all-white floral arrangement, or how dramatic your tables would look with just a bundle of white ostrich feathers tied with ribbon and placed in a clear vase surrounded by silver votive cups. Clear water-filled bowls with floating candles are super inexpensive and can be easily dressed up with a single floating rose or gardenia bloom. Low round or square vases filled with seashells make a charming touch to a seaside wedding, and lemons or limes stacked in tall glass cylinders are perfect for any summer reception.

Additionally, don't get stuck on the notion that every table has to be adorned the same way. Particularly if you're a fan of the tall, large breed of centerpieces, not every table requires the same spend to make an impact. In fact, your reception room can look even more interesting by putting your tallest centerpiece picks on a third of the tables, a smaller, less-pricey version on a third of the tables, and a combination on the remaining third.

Thing 32: Broaden your horizons and your bud-

get by looking beyond the traditional "wedding" flowers.

Peonies, calla lilies, certain roses, and all types of orchids do indeed scream "bride," but they also scream "expensive." Consider less-expensive options such as dahlias, zinnias, carnations, mums, tulips, hydrangea, and daisies for chic, tight little bouquets and lovely clusters for centerpieces. A country wedding can have an extremely lush look for little investment by using Gerber daisies in either all white or a variety of festive colors. Even baby's breath, which has been banished from stylish weddings for a while now, has made a comeback as a charming addition to tablescapes. Use bunches of baby's breath, lavender, or even fresh herbs to fill mint julep cups or short, clear vases for a sweetly chic touch. The key to making this technique look stylish is to use this type of greenery on its own without any other fillers, and to make the bunches tightly packed.

On the flipside, if you absolutely must become man

and wife amongst cymbidium orchids or grapefruit-sized peonies, minimize the splurge by having your bridesmaids carry a single, ribbon-tied stem and forgo extravagant centerpieces in favor of floating a single bloom in a water-filled vase or in a low bowl surrounded by floating candles.

Thing 33: Your money goes furthest with in-season flowers, preferably only one type.

Saving money by selecting only in-season blooms is such a simple premise, but few people other than florists actually know what flowers are in season during their wedding month. Streamline your research process by checking out floral reference Web sites, like the California Cut Flower Commission at ccfc.org, for guides on flower trends, wedding floral ideas, and flowers-by-season charts.

In general, year-round flowers include roses, lilies, carnations, orchids, delphinium, ranunculus, and stephanotis. In-season best buys for spring weddings include peonies, tulips, freesia, anemone, and daffodils. Summer-blooming favorites include azalea, hydrangea, iris, peonies, gardenia, and lily of the valley. Fall flowers include the ever-charming sunflowers, hydrangea, and jasmine. Winter blooms naturally include poinsettias but also freesia, rose gentian, and amaryllis.

Regardless of what kind of flower you choose, using just one type of flower everywhere can really stretch your budget. Truly beautiful floral arrangements don't necessarily have to incorporate a dozen different varieties of flowers in a spectrum of colors to look lush. Use one type of flower everywhere, from the bouquets to the table arrangements, for a trend-defying, elegant, monochromatic look. The budgetary beauty of this choice is that your florist can place one bulk order for your wedding, often at a much better rate than if you need a little of this and a little of that. Lest you think it will look uninspired, just think how stylish your reception room will look when it's bedecked in hundreds of creamy white tulips or lush, dinner-plate sized mums. There's nothing skimpy about that!

Thing 34: Cut centerpiece costs by providing your own containers.

The popularity of eclectic mixed decorating styles in home design and restaurants has crossed over to the wedding industry, and part of the beauty of this type of mismatched, one-of-a-kind style is that it doesn't have to be expensive to look utterly phenomenal. In fact, the opposite is true, with flea market finds like teapots and candlesticks adding fantastic punches of color and character to your tablescapes.

For a real bargain, look to what you already own (or can borrow from a relative) that's wedding-worthy. Got a collection of beautiful antique fruit bowls, gorgeous glass votive candleholders, or mint julep cups? Or are you willing to scout out the second-hand shops for interesting vessels like mismatched crystal vases, vintage juice glasses, ceramic water pitchers, or even china sugar bowls? You'd be surprised how much personality they bring to your event.

Whether you are doing the flowers yourself and need containers or want a cheaper alternative than having your florist provide them, scan the decorative accessories section of your favorite stores like Target, IKEA, Anthropologie, and Home Goods. Shop with your theme in mind whenever you're in one of these retailers, and you could easily score the perfect pewter or sterling silver serving bowls, antiqued gold candlesticks, or glass or ceramic vases that add the perfect touch to your flowers, for far less than renting containers from your florist. If your color palette happens to overlap the hues of any holiday or seasonal decor, such as jewel tones; red, green, and metallic gold of Christmas; black, silver, and gold of New Year's Eve; pink and red of Valentine's Day; or warm earth tones of fall, then you have it made. All of the above stores and countless more will have plenty of containers and other decorations that will look tailor-made for your event, both during the season and in the post-holiday markdowns. Online resources are invaluable as well, such as Etsy.com for unique, handmade items, and eBay for new and gently used housewares and party goods. You can even save cash while saving the earth by purchasing used or leftover party goods on EventLeftOvers. com, which has stellar steals on decorations of all kinds, from votives to centerpieces, as well as big-ticket items like old-school photo booths.

— 8 —

Down the aisle in style: your dress and accessories

— 8 —

Down the aisle in style: your dress and accessories

The amount of money that you choose to spend on your wedding gown and accessories is such a personal, fluid decision that it seems to defy the once-standard guidelines of allotting between 2 and 10 percent of your total wedding budget toward your "look." I've known brides with $60,000 wedding budgets who spent only a few hundred dollars on their wedding gown from a discount bridal superstore like David's Bridal or who struck gold at a 75-percent-off sample sale. And I've also known brides who had a $10,000 wedding budget who spent $3,000—30 percent of their total budget!—on her dream dress. Surprisingly, it's not always the fashionista brides who splurge the most on their gowns, either—gown greed can strike anyone.

In the past decade, the average price of a wedding gown skyrocketed faster than a bride could keep up. Bridal brands, once unrecognizable to the non-betrothed crowd, became bona fide fashion forces, with designers like Vera Wang, Badgley Mischka, and Monique Lhuillier becoming household names. Many style-conscious brides bought into the notion that an exquisite wedding gown had to cost several thousand dollars or more and be purchased from only the most exclusive, upscale bridal salons that required appointments and a six-month lead time. But there are other options for that anxiety-inducing scenario.

In response to the needs of today's recessionista brides, many top-tier bridal designers, including the powerhouses listed above, are actually producing secondary lines with lower price points. (Lower price point being a relative term, of course—we're still talking low four-figures here.) I'm not saying that it's making couture more accessible to the average bride, but it is a move in the right direction.

Thankfully, there are plenty of ways you can still wear a spectacular wedding gown without blowing a huge chunk of your wedding budget on it. The more time you give yourself to find the right gown, the more awesome yet affordable options you'll have, so try to give yourself at least a month or two to find the greatest steals.

Thing 35: Streamline the wedding gown search by first deciding upon your wedding date and time of day, the location, and the general size of your guest list.

The dizzying array of wedding gown styles can overwhelm even the most fashion-fluent bride. Do yourself a favor by making some key event decisions before you go dress shopping. For example, once you've decided to exchange vows in the middle of an apple orchard on a crisp October morning, followed by a country picnic-style lunch reception for thirty of your closest loved ones, it should be a lot easier to resist the ultra-fluffy and puffy ball gowns encrusted with Swarovski crystals and consider something a bit more understated. Well, at least I hope it is.

The budgetary benefit of this strategy is that if you go dress shopping before you've ironed out the other pertinent details (and their costs), it's easy to get so carried away with what you believe is the dress of your dreams that you'll go ahead and buy it . . . possibly spending far more than what makes sense for your wedding overall. Not to mention the headache of trying to plan a wedding that fits your dress style, rather than the other way around. I've seen brides race to the bridal boutiques practically the day they become engaged, and put down a deposit on a $7,000 gown before having any clue when or where the wedding will be or how much they really have to spend. I've always suspected that that's precisely how those brides with ten-grand budgets ended up with those $3,000 dresses.

Thing 36: When budgeting for your wedding gown, include additional costs such as alternations, underpinnings, and all of your accessories.

No matter how much the wedding gown costs, it's typical for the alterations to run $500 or more, even if all you'll need is a hem. That's a significant addition to what is most likely the most expensive item of clothing you'll ever buy.

Your dress could also require special underpinnings, which is bridal-speak for super-expensive wedding underwear like a specific type of corset, bustier, or slip. Most bridal salons will have the appropriate items available for sale, but you may be able to find the same or similar ones at a department store for a much lower price.

Accessories can be a huge money drain if you're not careful, so make sure you've budgeted for them rather than just buying them on a whim as you see things you love. It's easy to drop $75 on a pair of earrings here, $150 on a pair of shoes there, and $100 on a clutch purse, and next thing you know, you're several hundred bucks in and you've still got a headpiece and veil to shop for. That's how a bride can end up with $800 worth of accessories that were never in her dress budget.

Thing 37: Bridal fashion doesn't always have to come from a bridal salon.

It's no secret that putting the word *bridal* in front of something automatically raises its price exponentially. There's no rule that says your wedding shoes have to be purchased from a bridal salon; in fact, pick up a pair of gorgeous silver or gold metallic sandals and they will be wedding-worthy as well as a smart spend, since you can wear them for any other occasion. (Sadly, the same is just not true for those overpriced, blinding white satin pumps that so many bridal consultants push, assuring you that you'll dye them black and wear them forever. Maybe you will . . . and maybe you won't.)

Once you've purchased your gown, start scoping out your favorite department stores, local boutiques, and e-tailers for shoes as well as fantastic bridal-perfect jewelry, hair accessories, and purses, which will likely cost a fraction of their wedding counterparts, especially if you shop during sales.

Furthermore, even the dress of your dreams may not necessarily be a wedding dress. If your wardrobe is heavily stocked with fashion finds from J. Crew, Banana Republic, Nordstrom, Ann Taylor, or the ingenious online designer outlet bluefly.com, there is a good chance that you will be a fan of their selections of special occasion dresses, many of which come in white, ivory, or ultra-pale pastels. (The same companies are also fantastic resources for bridesmaids dresses and mother-of-the-bride attire, by the way.) Ann Taylor has become such a hot spot for bridesmaids dresses and informal wedding dresses that it recently launched its own wedding and event collection. (Check it out at anntaylor.com for fabulously fashionable, frugal dresses for your rehearsal dinner and bridal showers too!)

If your big day calls for a breezy white sundress, a festively chic cocktail dress, or a beautifully tailored ivory suit, check out the latest collections from Nicole Miller, Tahari, Rebecca Taylor, and Nanette Lepore at your favorite department or specialty store, or browse the special occasions section at Nordstrom or Nordstrom Rack. Brides are continually shocked at the treasures that can be found for incredible prices if they just expand their search beyond the bridal path.

And if beloved Vera is out of your price range but you're determined to walk down the aisle in a swoonworthy Wedding Gown with a capital "W," I'm continually impressed by J. Crew's exquisite collection of wonderfully contemporary wedding gowns, crafted of impeccable fabrics including ethereal silk chiffon, sculptural taffeta, fine French Chantilly and Alençon lace, delicate silk organza, and more. The overall feel is J. Crew sensibility tweaked with romantic and unique details, such as hand-rolled silk flowers, couture-quality trims, and flirty satin sashes. Prices start around $295 and range up to over $2,000, but even the most luxe gowns are far more affordable than other couture-look bridal brands. Consider it a great resource for bridesmaids dresses and flower girl dresses as well.

Thing 38: If you dream of a designer gown, signing up for the e-mail list on the Web sites of your favorite designers could equal significant savings.

Though bridal designers who have their own flagship stores do not normally run sales, join their e-mail list so that you can receive notices of all of their in-store events, including trunk shows, V.I.P. shopping events, and sample sales.
While designer trunk shows and V.I.P. events are not exactly "sales," many salons offer considerable incentives like throwing in a free veil with a gown purchase, and even discounts (usually 10 to 15 percent off) if you place your order on a certain date. In addition, these events are often rare opportunities to meet the designer and get his or her opinion of the

gowns you try on and get creative input on accessories too.

A designer sample sale can save you as much as 80 percent off of the retail price, and if you're incredibly lucky, you may get away with needing only minimal alterations and a decent dry cleaning, making it quite an amazing steal. However, across the board, all sales are final, which amps up the risk involved. Beware that some samples have been tried on literally hundreds of times by brides, likely have been shipped across the country several times from trunk show to trunk show, and may have been modeled several times in runway shows and at wholesale bridal markets before they reach that almighty sample sale. Thus, check over the dress extremely carefully for stains, snags or tears, broken zippers, torn linings, or other misdemeanors that may cost you a sizeable amount to have repaired. Also proceed with caution if the gown will clearly need some major alterations in order to fit you—it's typically easier and less expensive to take a dress down in size than to gain even a half-inch in size by letting out the seams. Anything more challenging than that should ideally be discussed with a seamstress before you purchase a final-sale gown.

Thing 39: You can get a pricey wedding gown without the wedding gown price!

Shopping for your wedding gown is an experience like no other, and nothing can match the giddy, exuberant atmosphere and full service of the best bridal salons. However, not every bride can afford salon prices. If your wedding gown budget just isn't giving you options at the bridal boutiques, there are many good alternative routes to getting you into that gown you've envisioned for your big day. So before you give up and decide to say "I do" in a fashion "don't," consider a less-traditional, less-costly avenue for gown shopping. With brides being more fiscally creative, they are suddenly buying pre-owned wedding gowns, purchasing through online discounters, going the vintage route, having gowns made, and even renting gowns more than ever before. Great deals do exist, that's for sure, but you must be an informed, thorough consumer to make sure that you know exactly what you're getting. No one wants to end up with a dress that doesn't fit, isn't in good condition, or is not what you thought you were getting. Keep the following guidelines in mind to avoid any dress regrets.

Pre-owned gowns are, next to pre-owned Hermes Birkin bags, one of the hottest commodities on auction sites like eBay and online shops like SavetheDress.com and WoreItOnce.com. And for good reason: a quick search of your preferred bridal designer's name will likely yield a shocking number of results, in all different sizes, all different styles, and all different prices, and if it doesn't, some sites even let you post your own ad describing the dress you're looking for so that sellers can respond. It certainly beats the legwork of scouting out sample sales, rental houses, or consignment shops in person, and you can even narrow your search by style name or style code if you have that invaluable information. But, as with all purchases in the Internet world, *caveat emptor* should be your guide. Make sure you've seen the gown in person at a salon so that you truly know what to expect. Read the seller's feedback score and history. Have all of their customers been happy? Make sure that they accept PayPal or another safe, protection-boosting, reputable form of payment, as opposed to requiring payment by cash, check, or money order. You can't read the gown description too many times or pore over the photos too closely. Make sure that every measurement is spelled out, and have a friend take your exact measurements to make sure the size is right, rather than going by "The gown is a size 6" or another equally vague statement. Study over every single detail of the seller's shipping rates and time frame, their return policy (which will probably be as succinct as No Returns), the gown measurements, and notes on any marks, stains, tears, or other imperfections. Don't hesitate to ask for additional photos or details and questions regarding where and when the gown was originally purchased, whether it has already been dry-cleaned, and how it has been stored. (For example, make sure that the gown has been stored in a canvas garment bag away from pets, smoke, and other potential allergens and odors.) Scope out other auctions for the same brand and style to see what price level the gowns are commanding, and don't get swept away by the excitement of a bidding war or a "Buy It Now" if the price is over your budget or you aren't truly ready to commit to buying the gown. If you're lucky enough to find the exact gown you've been pining for in near-mint condition, in your size, and the price is right, you just may become the proud owner of your dream gown. Make sure you've allowed plenty of time for the dress to arrive and be altered and pressed well before your wedding date, and once it does arrive, immediately check it for any defects so that you have time to communicate concerns with the seller. Then bask in the glow of owning that magnificent gown that you thought would never be attainable. Consider it a "green" statement and an example of recycling at its best!

Renting a wedding gown is becoming more and more popular, especially in larger metropolitan areas such as Los Angeles. Thanks to the declining economy, high-end wedding gowns are less accessible to the average bride, but their cachet and lust-worthiness have certainly not diminished, and savvy brides are finding that a rental can give them a lot more luxe for a lot less cash. As long as you are not overly sentimental and don't mind not being able to pass your wedding gown on to your own daughter someday, gown rental may be your best budget-boosting solution. Rental companies such as One Night Affair have a vast selection of styles and sizes from exclusive designers including Vera Wang, Amsale, Carolina Herrera, Monique Lhuillier, and many more, for a fraction of their original retail prices, starting as low as around $200. Some rental packages even include a veil and other accessories, for fashion styling in one easy step. Realize that only very minor alterations are allowed on a rental gown and that if you are typically hard-to-fit, it may be a challenge to find your dream gown in your correct size, so keep an open mind and try on many options. The good news is that no one would guess the gown's on loan—they are typically kept in extremely good condition, with no signs of having been down the aisle before. An additional plus is that after your wedding, there's no hassle or expense of having to pay for your gown to be cleaned, packed, and preserved for safekeeping, and you won't have to find a place to store it. Want karmic bonus points? Beam in the knowledge that, as with a pre-owned gown, you've managed to implement the recycle-reuse theme into your fashion statement.

A vintage wedding gown can make an incredible one-of-a-kind fashion statement, add a real sense of history and character to your wedding, and be a smart buy too. Whether you shop at an exclusive vintage boutique in a chic urban area or discover a hidden treasure at a flea market booth, the wedding gowns will be considerably more affordable than a new gown from a salon.

However, the hunt for just the right vintage dress is far more challenging than you might expect. One reason is that unfortunately, many vintage gowns just do not stand the test of time well enough to be deemed wedding-worthy, since some fabrics get slightly yellow as they age, some laces become stiff, and some once-invisible stains (like white wine or powder makeup) eventually darken over the years. When possible, avoid buying a gown that needs a dry-cleaning, as many of the old fabrics can be damaged by the chemicals used for cleaning today. If it's not avoidable, then at least be realistic about what a good dry-cleaning job can and can't undo as well as whether the fabric looks as sumptuous and crisp as it should. Buy from a seller who is knowledgeable about their gowns and ask if they can recommend a great dry-cleaner and alterations expert, if needed. Furthermore, the sizing of vintage gowns is a learning curve itself. Know that sizes have never been standard and have changed significantly over the decades. For example, a dress from the 1950s marked as a size 10 is actually closer to a size 6 in modern clothing. It doesn't help that women's bodies have gradually grown larger and more muscular too, so that the sleeves, shoulders, and waist circumference on many vintage styles are much smaller than on today's counterparts. And let's not overlook the various underpinnings that vintage styles required, like industrial-strength corsets to sculpt that retro hourglass shape. Though dresses with a generous seam allowance (at least a half-inch) are possible to let out, keep in mind that doing so may expose a portion of fabric that has, up to now, been hidden away in a seam and could be a slightly different color than the rest of the gown that has faded over time.

If you've found the holy grail of vintage gowns, one that's in great shape, fits well, or needs only minimal alterations and makes you feel like a million bucks, go for it! Again, ask for referrals of tailors and dry cleaners who specialize in vintage clothing. Make sure that the level of alterations and cleaning won't add an exorbitant cost to your gown and ruin the deal.

Online gown discounters are, for obvious reasons, a thorn in the side for the traditional brick-and-mortar bridal salons. It's tough for a full-service salon to compete with the low overhead and small number of staff that an online shop can operate with, and it's tough for a budget-conscious bride to overlook the significant savings the discounters offer. More problematic yet is the abundance of wedding gown scams or disreputable online shops that may be selling defective or even counterfeit designer gowns for as low as 75 percent off of the retail price! Sad but true, many a bride has been duped by a seemingly legitimate online shop and ended up with a wedding gown made of poorly sewn, cheap fabric, a weak imitation of her dream gown and an expensive lesson learned the hard way. For that reason, if you're thinking of buying your gown online, it's safest to choose a site that does have an actual brick-and-mortar location as well. You'll be able to check out their reputation and, if it's near where you live, you may be able to try on their dresses in person before buying online or having your alternations done in their store.

That being said, the allure of other types of dis-counters is potent, especially when your budget is limited, and even more so if you don't live in an area bustling with bridal salons offering myriad options and price points. So if you're considering the online route, you have to research, research, and research some more. Check out the Better Business Bureau in the state where the site is registered or check consumeraffairs.com/weddings for reports on the company. Verify that the site is selling authentic, new, unworn wedding gowns and not imitations of a designer's style or used gowns. And please, puh-*lease* make sure that you've seen the gown, or at least a very similar version of it by the same brand, in person at a salon before you jump in and order it. Even the highest-quality photos don't do dresses justice, and it's difficult to tell what a fabric, beading, trim, or even color will actually look like in person. When you start searching online, you need to know exactly what gown you want and what size to order it in. Have your measurements done by a friend (or, preferably, a professional seamstress) and order the appropriate size, always ordering up in size if your measurements fall within two parameters. Make sure that you are allowed to return the gown within a certain time frame if it doesn't fit. The bottom line is that yes, the savings of buying from an online discounter can be huge, but just be absolutely sure that you know what you're buying and who you're buying it from. Two suggested sites to check out are netbride.com and rkbridal.com, the online store for this New York City bridal shop.

Having your gown made has long been a popular alternative for brides who have a clear vision of the gown style that they want. Of course, even if you're dead-set on wearing a certain silhouette, say a strapless A-line gown, don't even think of securing a seamstress for your dress until you have tried on several dresses of this style and know how it looks on your body. What we love in magazine ads is seldom what we end up loving most in person, so do yourself a favor and try on different silhouettes either in a bridal salon or from a dressmaker's samples before you decide on "the one."

Additionally, be willing to spend quite a bit of time either purchasing the fabric and trimmings on your own or selecting from swatches that your seamstress may provide. Know also that a number of fittings, usually at least three but often more, will need to be fit into your schedule, just as you'd have several fittings for a gown purchased at a bridal salon.

Finally, don't assume that having a dress made will necessarily save you a bundle of money. The cost of making a wedding gown has many variables, including the area where you live, the experience level of the seamstress, the complexity of the gown you want, and the type of fabric you choose. Very roughly speaking, the starting price of having a custom-made wedding gown is around $500 and can easily surge from there, particularly if you want detailed work like hand-beading, embroidery, pleating, or other labor-intensive embellishments, or choose a fabric that's difficult to work with, such as velvet or a delicate lace.

If you choose to go this route, let the saying "you get what you pay for" be a running mantra in the back of your mind when you're researching dressmakers. Don't assume that a person who can make a fine party dress is automatically befit for the job of an elaborate wedding gown, and don't jump at a price that looks too good to be true without checking out all the details. Though a seamstress certainly doesn't have to work in a couture-caliber showroom or elaborate studio in order to be talented, don't overlook warning signs like work areas that are dirty, disorganized, and cramped. You absolutely *must* check out the portfolio and references of any seamstress you consider hiring, as well as get a full written contract that states the due date and the price of the gown, and whether that price includes a fixed or unlimited number of fittings, whether the price of fabric and trims is included, and any additional costs such as pressing or adding a bustle. Phew!

All of that being said, there are many benefits, economically and creatively, to having your gown made. For starters, most cities have an abundance of extremely talented, independent seamstresses who adore what they do and are nothing short of amazing. Many of them even worked for bridal companies or as in-house seamstresses or tailors for bridal salons before going on their own, and thus know all of the high-end techniques that make for couture-quality dresses that look outrageously expensive. Because the gown is made for you, the fit should be even more impeccable than one that has to be either taken in or let out for you. Finally, if you've got a creative bent, you may love the process of being able to coordinate your own fabric choices and add interesting, unique details to your gown instead of choosing someone else's design.

— 9 —

Wedding photography is always worth the splurge

− 9 −

Wedding photography is always worth the splurge

One thing that most wedding planners seem to agree on is that, regardless of the budget and size or scale of the wedding, photography is never the place to cut corners. Though the fees of professional wedding photographers can seem downright daunting, easily snapping up 10 to 15 percent of your overall budget, capturing those incredible once-in-a-lifetime moments truly is priceless. Long after the flowers have wilted and your veil has been tucked away into the corner of a closet, wedding photos can magically transport you right back to that one glorious day, no matter how many years have passed. It goes without saying that you want those precious visual reminders to be as beautiful, tasteful, and exquisite as possible, right?

Depending on what part of the country you live in, expect a photography package to start at a minimum of $1,000, with most brides spending above $4,000. For the typical wedding, a photographer will shoot between 1,000 and 2,000 pictures, and then may select around 500 of the best for you to choose from. Obviously, there is a huge spectrum of prices that couples will end up spending on their photography, depending not just upon the price your talented photographer commands but also on the types of images and album you select. However, no matter how much cash you can afford to invest in photography, some standard advice applies. Here are several insider tips to stretch your photo dollars.

Thing 40: No matter how tight your budget is, hiring the very best photographer you can afford is always money well spent.

When you look at photos of other weddings, think about the qualities that make a certain shot speak to you and touch your heart. Is it a great candid moment that reveals a great emotion? Is it a lighting technique? Is it a group shot that conveys real personality? Weddings are emotionally charged, time-sensitive events; think of them as somewhat akin to a fast-paced sporting event, where the timing of the right shot means either capturing the winning point, missing it altogether, or catching something in between. Those same split-second increments of your wedding day are the story you hope will be told by your wedding album and framed images that will flourish your home for a lifetime. And make no mistake, this level of artistry takes real talent and real experience to achieve, while a photographer with less finesse may rely on cheesy poses, have less chemistry with the guests, and have a limited creative point of view. Now is not the time to give a newbie a break—let him practice on someone else's wedding!

Many couples, feeling desperate from the ever-mounting financial pressures, can be tempted to hire a photography student or a well-intentioned and possibly even talented friend or family member to photograph the day. In my opinion, this is a riskier move than running with scissors. There's nothing worse than being stuck with a collection of photos that miss the mark on timing, are overlit, or are out of focus. Remember, you only get one chance at the moment that "I do" is said, one chance at that first slice of wedding cake. There are no do-overs.

If, for whatever reason, you think you've discovered the next Herb Ritts at the community college around the corner and you're set on hiring this new talent, it's wise to try a smaller "practice" assignment first so you can get a feel for what he really can deliver. Consider hiring him to shoot your engagement photo session or to take photos at your engagement party or bridal shower—basically, any occasion that will allow him to express his talent before your actual wedding is at stake. Additionally, stack the odds in your favor by having a friend act as backup for the photographer so you're sure that every important person and moment is captured by at least one of the two. Two amateurs are better than one, particularly if you'll have 100 or more guests.

Whether you canvass professional wedding photographers or more amateur ones, what you seek is a photographer whose work reflects the style you want, whether it's a fine-art look or a more candid, photojournalistic technique. You should look at examples of different types of weddings that he or she has shot, from casual beach weddings to black-tie affairs and at different times of day. Make sure the pictures show that the photographer was truly in the moment, capturing the mood and emotions of all the key moments of a wedding, showing glimpses of spontaneous joy that erupt during an event, from the bride getting dressed before the wedding to the ring bearer's giddy race down the aisle and the tears in a father's eyes as he walks his daughter down the aisle.

Everyone has budget constraints, and I would not tell any couple to go beyond what they can truly afford on any aspect of their wedding, including the photography. However, do allot as much money as you can to this vital category, even if it means that you borrow some funds from another, more ephemeral one, like your invitations, wedding favors, or other areas where it's easier to skimp a bit without anyone the wiser.

Sometimes, no matter how much creative budgeting you do, the photographer you love most is simply way out of your reach. If that's the case, then by all means ask them to recommend a peer they trust or perhaps a junior photographer within their studio if they have a large operation. Of course, you will still have to do your homework and check out the photographer's work and references yourself, but at least you've got a valuable starting point. If you're open and honest about your budget from the start and can articulate the type of style you want, you should be able to streamline your search without wasting any vendor's valuable time or getting your heart set on photography that is far above your budget comfort zone.

Thing 41: Up your buying power by prioritizing your photography wish list.

Whether your wedding will run under three hours start to finish or top out around six hours, you must make sure that your photo and video spend has the maximum impact. Well before the event, sit down with your fiancé and discuss what images are the most meaningful to you. Are you in love with formal bride-and-groom portraits? Is it important to have numerous intergenerational group shots that document your whole family? Do you want every moment of the reception captured on film, or can you put more money into the ceremony and cut back on the party pics? Everyone's tastes and needs are different, as are the dynamics of every family. But whatever your personal situation, there are many ways to make the most of even a very limited budget.

Though you'll likely be booking a minimum fixed number of shooting hours with your photography package, keep in mind that weddings do tend to run behind schedule. Decide what's most important to you so that your wishes are met without danger of having to pay overtime fees. For example, would you be content with professional photography of the pre-wedding prep and the ceremony, and let your guests document the reception by providing disposable cameras at each table so you'll get loads of candid shots? Or would you prefer to have your photographer shoot from the beginning of the ceremony through the early moments of the reception? Also, check your photo package agreement carefully to see if it includes any components that you may be able to "trade"—for example, swapping the formal portraits for an extra hour of reception photography.

If you do need a certain number of formal portraits, as in the different combinations of the bride and groom alone, each with their own families, the couple with their wedding party, the bride with her dad and Wife #3, and so on, be aware that this can be a time-consuming task for any photographer. Limit the number of portraits to those you care about most, and strongly consider having them taken before the ceremony begins. I know, I know, tradition dictates that the bride and groom don't see each other before the ceremony, but the fact is that many of today's couples are risking the potential for bad karma in order to get those posed shots out of the way. This allows them to spend precious time with their guests during the post-ceremony cocktail hour instead of spending that time in pose after pose. And romantic types, fear not: most photographers understand the significance of that first moment that the bride and groom see each other and have dramatic and creative ways for them to be "presented" to one another when this pre-wedding photo shoot takes place. That first moment you lock eyes will still be as breathtaking and memorable as if it happened on your walk down the aisle.

Thing 42: Buy a photo package that gives you the most freedom.

Don't stress over not being able to afford all of

the prints you want right away. When comparing photography packages, ensure that you have unlimited usage photo rights to all of your shots. Read that fine print on the contract carefully before you put down a deposit to make sure you won't have restrictions on how many prints or copies you can make from each image on your disc as well as on the time frame. This way, you can put off spending money for prints for a bit later when you've got the cash to do so.

Also, when you're on a budget, skipping the photographer's album service can save you big bucks. Today's couples have more creative and economical options than ever before, with the trend of do-it-yourself wedding albums going strong. A number of user-friendly, reasonably priced sites let you create your own wedding book with hundreds of different layout options, book sizes, and cover styles. Among the best sites to scout are blurb.com and MyPublisher.com. You can even choose to purchase only your proofs for now and craft a beautiful album out of

those, and order more prints or upgrade to a professional album later on when you can afford it.

Thing 43: Videography doesn't have to be a major spend.

Videography is a completely different animal
than wedding photography, and should be prioritized
accordingly. What that means is that this is a case
where, if you need to save money, you can enlist a
friend or family member to record your wedding.
It's still best to have two amateurs rather than one
filming everything.

If you choose to hire a professional videographer,
you can still cut down on the total cost by minimizing his number of shooting hours. As with your
photos, prioritize the time frames that matter most
to you, whether it's having a video record of your
bridesmaids helping you into your dress, the entire
reception down to the very last dance, or having
each guest (or each couple) record a special message
or congratulatory wish to you on camera.

Though not everyone can become an instant film editor, creative types can save a bundle by doing the film editing themselves with editing software like Pinnacle Studio and Adobe Premium Elements. This allows the couple to pay the videographer to shoot the raw, unedited footage to save on editing fees, which can be substantial.

– 10 –

Paper artistry:
invitations and stationery

Paper artistry:
invitations and stationery

The invitation that you choose sets the tone for your entire wedding, including its formality, its style, and even its color scheme. It's the first impression your guests will have of your nuptials, and you want it to convey just the right message.

Though a vital component of any wedding, the invitation is one item that brides have recently started to minimize costs on in a very significant way, in part due to the accessibility of high-quality home printers and luxurious papers for do-it-yourselfers, but also to the quick emergence of electronic (paperless) invitations from trendsetters like Evite.com.

With the explosion of e-vites used in lieu of paper invitations for birthday parties and baby showers, so changes the landscape of wedding invitations.

Though wedding professionals are divided into two camps—those in favor of the save-the-earth-one-tree-at-a-time "greenness" of e-vites for weddings, and those who find them inappropriate for even the most casual affair—what no one can argue is that this is a powerful recession-friendly trend that's not going away anytime soon. Regardless of whether you send e-vites for your wedding, it's perfectly appropriate and smart to create a wedding Web site that can be utilized by any guest who is computer-savvy enough to log on.

Though the e-vite option is an unquestionable budget saver, this chapter will focus on tips for cutting costs of traditional (paper) invitations and stationery.

Thing 44: With wedding invitations and stationery, less is more.

Dialing down the extravagance and cost of your invitations and wedding stationery certainly does not mean less style. In fact, it can mean more creativity, as some of the most unique, distinctive paper artistry is actually the least expensive to produce. So repeat after me: simplify, simplify, simplify. Forget about over-the-top or outrageously wasteful invitations, escort cards, place cards, menus, save-the-dates, and all of the other types of stationery items that a wedding involves. As with all types of wedding vendors, when hiring a professional stationer, do be clear about your budget right from the start, preferably even underestimating it a bit, and do comparison shop. Remember that thanks to the e-vite trend, printers are now more competitive than ever before.

Invitations are probably the first item that you'll choose, with all of the other stationery items taking style cues from it. Put the most money into the invitations, and cut corners by using less expensive papers and printing for the ancillary stationery like the table place cards, and consider even printing some of those less-significant items yourself. (More on doing it yourself in a minute!) No matter how much you've got to spend, it's so easy to wind up with an ultra-expensive invitation without having a clue of how you got to that price. The fact is that each element you choose, from the card stock or paper to the printing technique, and even the size of your invitation, affects the final price. So take it step-by-step and be aware of more economical alternatives for each component.

As you design your invitation from start to finish, keep in mind that although this first impression of your wedding does indeed need to be a strong, tasteful, and stylish one, it really is the wedding that your guests will remember forever, not your invitation. That mindset will, I hope, keep you from veering too far into the extreme price-points as you go through the following steps.

Printing prices: First, you'll have a variety of printing methods to choose from, depending on how you want your invitation to look and how much you can spend. Engraving, the raised-lettering and indented back surface, is the most expensive type of printing and doesn't make much sense when you're on a budget. More economical printing methods are letterpress, which is best for a heavy paper or card stock, thermography, which uses a mixture of wet ink and resin powder to form raised lettering and is far cheaper than engraving, and finally offset printing, also called lithography, which is flat lettering and the least expensive method.

Type of paper: The most expensive type of paper is made of 100 percent cotton, which is the smoothest surface. A more economical choice is linen stock, which is also made of cotton but has a textured surface, like linen fabric. The use of translucent papers, such as parchment or cotton vellum, is a beautiful trend that makes for quite interesting invitations; however, keep in mind that these filmy types of papers will most often need to be attached to a heavier cardstock rather than used alone. Therefore, you'll need to price out the least expensive cardstock in order to keep your cost from skyrocketing.

Invitation style: Though you may be tempted to go with the more interesting custom-sized invitations and envelopes, keep in mind that with custom comes extra cost, from the more labor-intensive cutting down to the extra postage that's usually required with a nonstandard envelope size or shape. Whether you go with a single panel, bifold, trifold, or other type of invitation, stick to the "standard is best" rule to stretch your stationery dollars furthest.

Skip the extras, save a tree, and stay on budget: Cringe at the wastefulness of the traditional wedding invitation package and make a green (as in earth-friendly and cash-friendly) statement with your stationery. The least expensive invitation to make and mail is a single-panel invitation card in a standard size, with just an outer envelope. Seriously, skip over all of the extraneous upgrades like fancy tissue overlays, a colored envelope lining, a separate invitation envelope (which is placed inside of the outer addressed envelope), and heavy stock for the RSVP cards. A great way to save on money on the RSVP cards is to use a postcard in a paper stock that looks similar to but costs less than your invitation.

You won't need to pay for envelopes, and the postage is cheaper than a first-class letter stamp.

Create a wedding Web site to post details like maps, directions, and accommodations information: There's no need to waste money and paper to give out information that your guests will likely misplace by the wedding day anyway. Use a free wedding Web site to post hotel recommendations, weather updates, and other information for out-of-town guests. Free wedding sites include eWedding.com and Mywedding.com, while fee-based wedding sites include Wedshare.com and Wedsimple.com.

. . . And all the rest of your stationery package: The array of other paper items that you use on your wedding day is really up to you and your budget constraints. The bare bones essentials, besides the wedding invitation, are simply seating cards to indicate the guest's table at the reception. Further along on the wedding paper trail are items that are typically used at today's weddings but are not at all required. These include save-the-date cards, which

are of particular usefulness if your wedding will take place near a major holiday or any other time that's a popular travel time, if you're having a destination wedding, or if you have a large number of out-of-town guests that will need as much advance notice as possible in order to secure affordable flights. Also common are wedding programs, which can be as simple as featuring the names of all of the wedding party members or as elaborate as including the story of how the two of you met or expressing gratitude for anyone who played a special part in making your wedding day a success. Place cards, which designate each guest's specific seat at their reception table, are not only less commonly used, but can entail a huge hostess headache as you try to map out who sits where. Menu cards are also less common and are typically used only if you're serving either a very formal dinner or unusual and complex dishes for which you would like to detail the ingredients, types of sauce, or other interesting foodie-facts.

Thing 45: If you're crafty, consider do-it-yourself invitations, but know the hidden costs.

Making your own wedding invitations and stationery can certainly save you a ton of money if you do it right. However, as with making your own floral arrangements, wedding gown, or party favors, you have to be aware of the hidden costs of a do-it-yourself (DIY) project. For one, the time commitment alone is a major cost. Is it realistic that you can devote many evenings, middle-of-night hours, and weekends wrangling with your computer and printer, stuffing all of the envelopes, and addressing them? Do you have the time to shop in stores or online for paper stock? Additionally, do you already own high-quality, reliable equipment like a paper cutter and a great home printer that is able to handle heavy paper or card stock if that's what you plan to use? Do you already own interesting fonts on your software, or are you happy with the choices you can download for free?

I'm not trying to discourage anyone from DIY, but be honest about your skill and patience levels before you take on something as important as your wedding, especially considering that you'll be committed to making fifty or a hundred or two hundred of them. Have you had success in duplicating crafty things shown in photos before? Have you worked with paper crafts before? Are you good at following instructions? Sadly, though I fancy myself a creative type, when it comes to crafts, I end up with, at best, a clumsy, mediocre version of whatever charming little craft I've attempted. Based on my own track record, I now know that by the time I mess up each project numerous times, repurchase the supplies, and redo the whole monstrous mess, I've spent triple the retail price of ready-made items anyway.

That being said, if you are the lucky soul who possesses amazing craft finesse, has the free time to devote to it, and has a few willing friends to pitch in, then by all means, make your own invitations and stationery items and enjoy the smugness that comes from creating something truly unique and economical. There are still different levels of DIY to choose from. If you're particularly artsy, you can buy blank card stock and design your own original invitation, limited only by your imagination. Check out local stores as well as comprehensive online sites such as paper-source.com, dickblick.com, and mygatsby.com for amazing selections of paper and cards in all weights, colors, and sizes as well as artist's supplies and DIY kits. If your creative side is a little less evolved than, say, a certain Ms. Stewart, you can still create fantastically personal stationery without risking your sanity. Many stationery sites, such as 123print.com, are one-stop shops that allow you to design your own card or modify an existing one as well as purchase the paper and supplies. Alternatively, you can purchase a design software kit that includes a huge range of fonts and design templates that you can customize. A great example to check out is the Complete Wedding Publisher Software on ed-it.com, which costs under $30.

− 11 −

Wedding favors: say it with sugar

– 11 –

Wedding favors: say it with sugar

There has been a degree of controversy as of late regarding wedding favors. The debate is over whether they are a necessary evil or simply an extravagance that our wasteful and economically challenged culture would welcome a break from. Many couples have decided to eliminate wedding favors altogether, even when money is not an object. And when you do have to be cost-conscious, I can't think of a better budget line item to scale down than wedding favors, so do yourself a favor and don't overthink them, forget about going over-the-top, and definitely don't overspend on them. Times are tough, and in a world where decluttering is a national obsession, selecting a wedding favor that your guests will actually want to keep and use is harder than ever before.

I know you may have your heart set on favors of the precious sort, like the monogrammed wind chimes, little salt and pepper shakers with your names and wedding date, and all the other souvenirs that seem irresistible . . . but only to you. Let's face it, most of us are drowning in so much stuff that finding a place for yet one more useless—sorry, but engraving alone does not render an item useful—memento of someone else's wedding is low on the priority list. Should you decide to save some money and effort and skip over favors altogether, rest assured that your guests will not notice. Just ask any bride who did painstakingly select and pay dearly for lovely, meaningful wedding favors only to find half of them left behind on the dinner tables at the end of the night.

Thing 46: If you want to lavish your guests with favors, make them of the edible sort.

If allowing your guests to leave empty-handed just feels wrong, then by all means indulge your inner hostess-with-the-mostess, but skip the trendy trinkets and send your guests home with a simple but scrumptious, comfort-food-esque confection with universal appeal. After all, no matter how many outrageously indulgent bites your guests devoured during your wedding, you can bet they'll welcome a bedtime snack of homemade gourmet cookies from your favorite local bakery when they get back to the hotel, or a Chinese take-out container filled with candy for the long plane trip back home.

If you're lucky, you won't have to look further than your own family for a phenomenal baker with a good heart, a cherished recipe for lemon gingersnaps, and nothing but time on her hands. But even if Grandma doesn't know a brick oven from a bricklayer, or your family's version of homemade means putting Oreos on fine china, you can still bid your guests farewell with something that tastes homemade. Check out your favorite local bakeries for cookies or baby tarts or a confectioner like See's Chocolates, Fannie Mae, or Ethel M that offers reasonably priced chocolates that can be ordered in bulk. You can do the packaging yourself by simply placing each treat in a clear cellophane bag, tying it up with a ribbon, and patting yourself on the back. Check out Michaels craft stores and papermart.com for a huge variety of cello bags, miniature bakery boxes, favor boxes, and every type of ribbon known to man.

One of the best wedding favors I have received was charming, cheeky, and cheap. It was given at a summer backyard wedding with an old-timey retro theme, complete with old-fashioned lemonade and a daisy-covered wedding cake. The wedding favors cost less than $2 each and were a huge hit: red-and-white-striped popcorn boxes filled with nostalgic candies like root beer barrels, licorice pipes, candy buttons, and buttery caramels. If a retro charm doesn't fit your event style, you could fill boxes with your own childhood favorites, like Pop Rocks and Hubba Bubba. Though throwback candies aren't always easy to find, they are stocked by Cost Plus

World Market stores and many bulk candy Web sites including oldtimecandy.com and candywarehouse.com. DylansCandyBar.com, the high-end sweet-tooth boutique, also offers nostalgic candy as well as kitschy, wedding-perfect treats like the His-and-Hers Marital Bliss Milk Chocolate Bar.

Cheaper still is a bulk order of M&Ms, and I've yet to meet a person who can resist a beribboned bag filled with them. They are such an easy and inexpensive way to incorporate your wedding colors into favors and, for a bit more, you can have them emblazoned with an image for a true conversation starter. Order online at mymms.com.

A trend that can add a fun and interactive element to your favors is to make a candy table or candy bar for guests to make their own mix of sweets. It looks great in your reception photos, too, if you design it right. The main thing is to think of these favors as a stylistic element to your reception, and put some thought and creativity into the packaging and the display, particularly if you decide to go the candy table route. Just as you wouldn't toss a pack of gum at each place setting and smugly cross "FAVORS" off of your to-do list, you shouldn't put a muddled assortment of containers and colors on a table and expect it to look dazzling.

The most eye-catching idea is to go with one of the central colors in your wedding palette, whether it's pink, red, yellow, or even brown, black, or white, and create a striking sweets table out of candies in only that color. If one solid color choice isn't for you, think of another unifying element, such as placing the candies in a collection of white milk glass vases and dishes or a variety of antique water pitchers or crystal bowls—any type of object that adds style and character is great, and if it can easily be found at local flea markets or thrift stores, then even better. No matter what you choose, the key is to make sure that the containers look unified—even the most inexpensive, plain, clear glass jars, vases, and bowls look chic when filled with colorful candies. Vessels look best in various sizes, shapes and heights. Create dimension by placing the containers atop blocks of Styrofoam or empty boxes of different sizes that are hidden beneath your table linen. Classic, inexpensive glass containers and old-fashioned apothecary jars can be found at stores like Target, Michaels, and Bed Bath & Beyond. Metal scoops for the containers can be found at kitchen stores or restaurant supply stores.

With a bit of thought, you'll come up with a zillion other treats that can also make wonderful favors. Think locally, too—maybe your zip code is famous for a certain orange-spice scone or lavender-infused honey, or maybe an iconic candy is manufactured right around the corner. And if not, brainstorm with your fiancé and incorporate your shared favorite indulgences—the type of fortune cookie that held your wedding ring when he proposed, or the flavor of Girl Scout cookies you sold to him when you were twelve—to create a wedding favor that tells a story as well. I can practically guarantee that it won't end up in anyone's trashcan or donation bin.

— 12 —

Bridesmaids gifts: choose personality over price

~ 12 ~
Bridesmaids gifts:
choose personality over price

If you've ever been a bridesmaid yourself, you've probably received a few of the cliché bridal party gifts, like the ubiquitous strand of fake pearls or the chipped crystal box that didn't quite survive the long drive back home. Now it's your turn to select thank-you gifts for your bridesmaids and put some time and thought into what would really honor your friendship and their unique personalities rather than buying the typical "one-size-fits-all" selection of bejeweled photo frames and engraved keychains at many bridal salons and gift boutiques. The best part is that unique and meaningful does not have to mean pricey.

Celebrity brides have so overindulged their bridesmaids that the rest of us feel tragically cheap if we can't compete. We've all seen the magazine photos of a group of bridesmaids all decked out in matching "Bridesmaid"-emblazoned velour track suits, jeweled flip-flops and tank tops (the bridesmaids' gift of choice at celebutante weddings of the last decade), but you'll need at least $100 per girl in your gift budget to match that idea. Instead, spend half that amount and double the personality by giving each bridesmaid something that you've picked out just for her.

Thing 47: Bridesmaids gifts don't have to break the bank; think fun and personal.

Although traditionally a bride bestowed all of her bridesmaids with the same gift, it's not a rule. While you absolutely must be favoritism-free and make sure the gifts are all of equal value, tailoring your gift to each bridesmaid's own style, taste, and interests means that you can get as creative as you like. One way to carry out the "separate-but-equal" idea is to use one unifying element, say starting with the same cute but inexpensive tote bag for each girl, and then personalize them by filling them with different things.

A few examples: your beauty-junkie bridesmaid will flip over an assortment of luxury lotions and potions and a travel-sized set of quality makeup brushes; your bookworm bridesmaid would love a bundle of new fiction releases and a beautiful coffee-table book on her favorite subject; and your beach-babe bridesmaid will squeal over a cute pair of flip-flops, a beautiful sarong, and a collection of luxury sunscreens. You get the idea.

You could also choose a beautiful item that comes in an array of colors and styles, again going with the same yet different principle. Jewelry, such as a stunning pair of drop earrings with gemstones of different colors, is always happily received, as is a clutch purse or cosmetics case that can be used during the wedding and for other events.

If many or all of your bridesmaids will be traveling to come to your wedding, what better way to say thank you than to up the glamour quotient of their hotel stay by gifting them with ultra-luxe travel treats, like a bottle of wine and a box of chocolates or a basket of sumptuous bath and body products wrapped up in a fluffy robe or a cozy throw.

Most importantly, regardless of how much you spend on the gift, make sure that it includes a hand-written and heartfelt note that expresses your gratitude for your friend's help with the wedding as well as for your special friendship. Once your wedding photos are back, make sure that each bridesmaid is mailed a photo of the two of you together, which she's sure to cherish longer than any material gift you could buy.

~ 13 ~

Bridal beauty: when to go pro

— 13 —
Bridal beauty: when to go pro

When it comes to beauty, we do indeed live in interesting times. Just consider all of the complicated, exaggerated, and ultra-expensive beauty trends of late, hair straightening and hair extensions, eyelash extensions (!), and spray-on tanning, to name but a few. And it seems that some women want to sport it all—and all at one time—which equals overkill. (Sorry, *Real Housewives of New Jersey.*) As a lifelong beauty junkie, I'm always interested in the innovations, yet I seem to always ditch the trendy gimmicks in favor of looking groomed yet uncontrived and, I hope, timeless. After working with so many brides over the years, I can honestly say that every bride looks absolutely beautiful when she's walking down the aisle—seriously, if that glow could be bottled, I'd be bathing in it. And yet it's the brides who looked the most like themselves, as opposed to the perfectly polished yet virtually unrecognizable ones, who truly looked the best. I understand all too well how easy it is to get caught up in the "makeover mindset" and try to completely transform your look via loads of makeup and reams of hair extensions, but I hope that you'll consider going for a more natural look when you walk down the aisle. After all, it's nearly impossible to look timeless if you've bought into every trend in the book. Seriously, your wedding photos will soon look so dated that they may as well be stamped with "2:09 P.M., May 26, 2011" across your face.

No matter what you can afford to spend in the beauty department, consider how you'd look in your wedding gown if you resisted the costly, contrived treatments and products and instead tried a simpler, classic beauty look—what magazines famously call a "makeunder." If you're willing to experiment, try the following tips and see if you like the results.

First of all, forget the outdated rule that you have to do more for wedding beauty, like achieving freakishly big hair and using darker, bolder lipstick than you would ever wear in normal life. I, for one, am thrilled at the sea of change from the stiff, towering, upswept hair to long, loose waves. In fact, I think one of the most beautiful trends over the past several years is that brides are looking a lot less scary (buh-bye, contouring powder and dark lip liner!) and much more natural.

Instead of looking costumey in overly dramatic makeup colors, try using a different formula of your favorite color instead for a foolproof way to up the glamour score without going overboard. For example, you can stick to a rosy-pink blush, but try it in a slightly shimmering version if you always use matte, or amp up your berry-hued lipstick by going for a glossy finish if you normally wear a cream one. You'll still look like yourself, but with a more festive, polished twist.

Second, go against the grain of every magazine ad and ditch the dewy, shiny finish for your wedding day. Yes, it looks all sexy and glowy in a magazine, but unfortunately, in real life it just looks plain oily. You can still go for a glow, but a toned-down version that starts with oil-free moisturizer and foundation and takes on a luminous finish with the addition of subtle shimmer on your cheekbones, brow bone, down the center of your nose, and patted right on top of the cupid's bow above your lip. And take note, shimmer does *not* mean glitter. Fans of glitter can sprinkle it into oblivion for other events (maybe the bachelorette party), but *please* skip it completely for your wedding. I beg of you.

Thing 48: If you're into a natural-looking, "you-but-better" bridal beauty look, doing your own hair and makeup can be a smart savings.

If you agree that bridal beauty does not necessarily have to mean heavy makeup and elaborate, sculptural hairstyles, we're getting somewhere. The best part about the whole less-is-more look is that it's really quite user-friendly, even to take it up a notch for your wedding. If you're adept at creating your own beauty look for everyday wear and have no aching desire to completely transform your appearance just because you're a bride, then go for it.

Do, however, practice some extra-credit beauty maneuvers before your big day, like having your brows professionally shaped, and getting your hair trimmed of any split ends. Also take an inventory of your beauty arsenal to see whether you've got the necessary makeup formulas and colors that are long-lasting and appropriate for photos. For example, you'll want to use an oil-free, long-wearing foundation that won't sweat off, slide off, or rub off during the reception as well as a long-lasting yet nondrying lip color, plus waterproof eyeliner and mascara. Shop for the items you don't have either at a makeup counter where you can possibly glean a few application tips from the salesperson, or at a beauty mecca like Sephora, where you'll get advice as well as be able to try on products before you buy. Once you decide on the hairstyle you'll wear, also make sure you've got all the supplies you'll need to create it, like a high-quality blowdryer or flat iron, curling irons, hairpins, and a long-lasting hairspray. That being said, if your vanity drawer contains little more than ponytail holders, two-year old mascara, and some crumbles of powder blush, you may be in for an overwhelming and expensive shopping trip.

When that's the case, hiring a professional make-up artist and hairstylist, or someone who's adept at both, can save you a bundle on all those beauty products. The fee for wedding beauty services varies widely depending on where you live and the experience of the artist, but in general, expect to spend over $100, and even more if you plan to keep him or her around for touch-ups during the reception. (Unless the paparazzi are stalking your wedding, touch-up service would be the first thing to go if this was my budget on the line. Spend $5 on blotting papers to blot any excess oil and shine throughout your party and stash them and your lip color in your clutch for later, or ask a bridesmaid to hang on to them for you.)

If you're happy with your regular hairstylist, chances are you'll be able to hire him or her for your wedding. The makeup gig can be tougher to fill though, especially if you don't live near a big city that's packed with talented freelance makeup artists. However, you may be able to hire a makeup artist through your favorite department store cosmetics counter. Find a brand that you like, then scout out the salespeople at its counter with the intent of finding one who has a makeup style you can relate to—as in not overdone, tacky, or suited for a tween girl. Many of these sales consultants also work as freelance makeup artists in their off-hours, so it can't hurt to ask if they are available for hire.

Thing 49: Investing in the most effective bridal beauty regimen saves you money in the long run, regardless of the price.

When is an expensive product a smart splurge? When it's so effective that you don't need to get professional facials in order to get the best clear, glowing skin. Or when it's so concentrated that you only need to use a tiny amount and one container seems to last forever, like with the best concealers, blushes, and wrinkle-diminishing creams. I wish I could say that creating the most results-oriented routine for wedding-perfect makeup and skincare could be done on the cheap. But the fact is that after testing thousands of products in every price point, the best of the best beautifiers are all over the map in terms of price. There are some drugstore brands that are so fantastic that I'm forever loyal to them, some triple-digit-priced products that disappoint, and many hits and misses in between. So the best strategy is to give yourself as much time as possible prior to your wedding to try out a variety of products and brands because—and this is vital—you should *never* try out something for the first time the night before your wedding, whether it's a chemical peel, a self-tanner, or even a new conditioner for your hair. Evil things have a way of happening when you mix "biggest day of your life" with a big dollop of "miracle cream" and you could wake up to a red, oozing mess where your face used to be. Enough said? Just take some time and see what works best for you—which may be completely different than what works best for me, or your best friend, or your facialist, or whatever actress is on this month's cover of *InStyle* magazine.

The results of my unending, unbiased, yet wholly unscientific quest for the best beauty-makers for brides include the following staples.

1. A skincare problem-solving product that gets your skin in the best condition possible. Good skin translates to needing a lot less makeup in the first place. For the double whammy of blemish-fighting and wrinkle-diminishing powers, nothing beats retinol. Among my favorites is RoC Correxion Deep Wrinkle Night Cream (drugstore.com). I'm amazed by the fast results of Sunday Riley Juno Serum (barneys.com), perfect for people with dry skin, those prone to irritation, and even sufferers of eczema. Prepare to be sticker-shocked, but it actually cured the chronic dry patches on my face and hands after just two nights of using it.

2. *A lightweight, oil-free moisturizer to wear under foundation for your wedding.* Neutrogena Moisture Oil-Free is a frugal-yet-fabulous staple in my medicine cabinet. Even if you're usually dry, don't use anything oil-based on your wedding day—it will eventually slide off or melt off long before the bouquet toss.

3. *An eye cream that addresses fine lines, dark circles, and puffiness to lessen the effects of chronic sleep deprivation (a side effect of being engaged!).* Among my favorites is Nutritioniste Ultra-Lift Anti-Wrinkle Firming Eye Cream (drugstore.com). Make sure your eye cream and concealer blend well together and don't cake up.

4. A concealer that's neither too drying nor too creamy to blur undereye shadows, conceal blemishes, and temporarily erase redness, sun spots, and scars. It's not cheap, but Benefit Erase Paste (sephora.com) is worth its weight in gold. The teeny-tiniest dab is all you'll need, so you won't have to restock for quite a long, long time.

5. An oil-free, long-wearing liquid foundation. Priced at under $8, Rimmel London's Stay Matte Clarifying Foundation (target.com) blends and stays on as beautifully as foundation that cost quadruple its price.

6. Translucent loose powder to set your makeup and keep shine at bay. Laura Mercier Translucent Loose Setting Powder (lauramercier.com) is exactly what powder is supposed to be: silky, mattifying, and invisible.

7. A cream blush if your skin's at all dry or a powder blush for everyone else. Skip the difficult-to-blend gel and liquid blushes and try Bobbi Brown Pot Rouge (bobbibrowncosmetics.com), L'Oreal

True Match powder blush (drugstore.com), or a combination of both formulas for iron-clad long wear.

8. Waterproof eyeliner and mascara . . . even if you'll only use it just this once. Waterproof typically means drying, so I don't recommend using it for every day, but cry-proof eye makeup is a must-have for your wedding. Lancome (sephora.com) and L'Oreal (drugstore.com) consistently make outstanding waterproof versions of their mascaras and liners.

9. A long-wearing cream eyeshadow paired with a powder shadow. I think I've told every woman I know how much I love Bobbi Brown Long-Wear Cream Eye Shadows (bobbibrowncosmetics.com). There's not a loser color in the whole selection, they go on beautifully, and they really stay on all day long. You can make the color more intense by layering it on or by simply pairing it with a powder shadow on top. NARS (sephora.com) makes silky, subtle-to-smoky shadows in every color under the sun.

10. A brow powder-wax combo to darken brows and keep them in place. I'm a fan of the Urban Decay Brow Box Kit (beauty.com) which contains two shades of brow powder for custom blending, grooming wax, and the most precise Lilliputian tweezers known to man.

And, finally, consider your fragrance to be the ultimate wedding day accessory. Not only does the act of dabbing on a few precious drops of an exquisite perfume make anyone's serotonin soar, but it's scientifically proven that scent is one of the most powerful connections we have to our memories. Take care in choosing the scent that you'll wear when you walk down the aisle. For the rest of your life, the faintest trace of it can instantly transport you back to that moment. Though I have an addiction problem with custom-blended scents (and there's no twelve-step program for that just yet), admittedly, they can be wildly expensive. Less expensive fragrances that feel just as exclusive and one-of-a-kind can be found within niche brands such as L'Artisan Parfumeur (artisanparfumeur.com), Memoire Liquide (studio-beautymix.com), and Ebba (ebbalosangeles.com).

— 14 —

Haute honeymoons with hot deals

– 14 –

Haute honeymoons with hot deals

E very couple sees the honeymoon part of the wedding festivities in their own light. For some, cutting down the typical weeklong honeymoon by a couple of days brings the cost down enough so that they can have their (wedding) cake and eat it too. But for others, the honeymoon is even more important than the actual wedding, and they will gladly skimp on wedding details rather than skimp on (or even worse, postpone) the honeymoon even a little bit. Many of these couples decide on a destination wedding, so they can have the honeymoon of their dreams while spending their wedding budget on the things they care about most with the people they care about most.

Other couples want to splurge on a once-in-a-lifetime honeymoon trip but aren't fans of the destination wedding idea. If you fit into this category, there are ways to stretch your honeymoon budget, even if the economy isn't doing you any favors. For one, become a regular on the major discount travel sites like Expedia, Orbitz, Hotels.com, and AllLuxuryHotels.com as well as the Web sites for individual hotels that are on your wish list. Register on their e-mail list to stay up-to-date with any special offers and package deals. Take smart honeymooning further by looking into the following bargain-friendly strategies.

Thing 50: Keep your honeymoon trip close to home to cut out airfare costs altogether.

Let's face it, even if you score a great airline deal, flying is still costly. No matter where you live, there's likely to be a romantic getaway spot—whether it's a quaint inn or a secluded spa or an elegant city hotel—within reasonable driving distance.

Consider taking a quick, two-or-three-day road trip right after your wedding to decompress, celebrate your new life together, and get some much-needed rest before you dive right back in to the daily grind. This "mini-moon" is a great way to award yourself some newlywed-style pampering without a great expense. And remember, you can always take a longer, more exotic honeymoon later on, after you've had the chance to save up some money and accrue a few more vacation days from work.

Thing 51: A cruise or an all-inclusive resort can stretch your honeymoon dollars as well as your sanity.

The all-inclusive trip is a honeymooner's dream, offering no-surprises pricing, super-easy planning, and often at a lower price than a comparable standard trip. The trend of all-inclusive honeymoons has grown by leaps and bounds in the past couple of years and will surely continue to do so as their many happy recessionista brides sing their praises.

Whether a cruise or an all-inclusive resort, there are packages tailor-made to fit a variety of budgets and cover the majority of your expenses, from airfare, ground transportation, and accommodations to meals and entertainment.

All-inclusive chains like Sandals and Beaches (sandals.com and beaches.com) are the best-known, but there are numerous other companies that produce fantastic honeymoons on a budget as well. Check out classicvacations.com or honeymoonsinc. com for ideas and packages, or simply do a Google search on "all-inclusive" and your preferred destination for a dizzying array of options.

Thing 52: A honeymoon registry is a practical, tasteful route to instant gratification.

When setting up your wedding gift registry, be sure to consider the increasingly popular honeymoon registry, which may be a better fit for your lifestyle and needs at this moment. If a sumptuous honeymoon suite at a tropical resort is much higher on your priority list than cut crystal goblets and embroidered linens, you are not alone. Many couples are putting their short-term need—a romantic, memorable honeymoon—at the top of their wish list and deciding that those fancy high-ticket items like twelve place settings of fine china can wait until sometime down the road when they can afford the investment and may be more likely to use it.

If you and your future husband have already been living together before the wedding, it's likely that you've got the basics covered—an apartment or house that's pretty-well-appointed with plenty of dishes and towels and a decent coffeemaker—and honeymoon help would make a more useful gift than duplicate housewares.

Of course, some of your guests will feel that showing up to your wedding or bridal shower without an actual boxed and beribboned gift is akin to public indecency, and will prefer to shop off of a traditional list. That's fine, too, and you can certainly register at your favorite home store in addition to the honeymoon registry. Simply take an inventory of what you've already got, what needs to be replaced, and what you truly need, and compile a very practical, well-edited gift registry.

So just how exactly do you register for a honeymoon? Many major travel companies, such as resorts and cruise lines, offer their own registry service and will be happy to help you plan a gift list that fits your dream trip and your budget. However, be aware that independent registries, including the popular honeymoonwishes.com and honeyluna.com, will offer you greater flexibility and trip options than a single resort. As soon as you've decided on a honeymoon destination and a registry service, you can break your trip up into categories, so that your guests can contribute to a specific item, say dinner and champagne on the beach from the resort's restaurant, one night of your honeymoon suite, a couple's spa day, a snorkeling trip, or whatever you choose.

When considering a registry Web site, read all of the details and fine print. It's not a free service, and the company will charge a fee of up to 9 percent (sometimes even more) to cover the registry management, customer service support, and the Web site's hosting services. Find out whether this fee is deduced from your total gift tally, or if it's an additional charge tacked onto your guest's purchase. For example, a guest may choose to purchase a $100 portion of your airfare but will be charged a total of $109.

Also check whether the site works with a certain travel agency and requires you to book your trip through it. Using their preferred agency isn't necessarily a bad thing, since you may be eligible for special discounts that you would not have access to otherwise.

Conclusion

Conclusion

There you have it, 52 Things that I hope will inspire and guide you as you plan your wedding on a budget. Regardless of the state of the economy or your own personal spending cap, remember that money is not the greatest influence on style—your creativity is. Don't let financial frustration push you into costly decisions you may regret later, like going into debt to pay for the wedding.

At any stage of the wedding planning, if you're feeling that your vision is far beyond your budget's reach, take a step back for a moment and try to see your dream from another angle. Think outside the box, and you're likely to find a lot of options that not only help you make your dream a reality, but may even lead you to a new dream altogether. Let your own creativity—and this book—empower you to make the changes that can slash a few zeros off of your expense sheet without sacrificing an ounce of style. And do keep in mind that, as the years go by, your favorite wedding memories will most likely be of the things that money can't buy, like the swish of your dress as you danced with your new husband, your mother's tear-filled toast, or the sound of the waves as you exchanged vows on the beach. Those are the priceless moments that you'll treasure for a lifetime, long after the last vendor has been paid.

Notes

Check out these other books in the
Good Things to Know series:

5 Things to Know for Successful and Lasting Weight Loss
(ISBN: 9781596525580, $9.99)
12 Things to Do to Quit Smoking
(ISBN: 9781596525849, $9.99)\
20 Things To Know About Divorce
(ISBN: 9781596525993, $9.99)
21 Things To Create a Better Life
(ISBN: 9781596525269, $9.99)
27 Things To Feng Shui Your Home
(ISBN: 9781596525672, $9.99)
27 Things To Know About Yoga
(ISBN: 9781596525900, $9.99)
29 Things To Know About Catholicism
(ISBN: 9781596525887, $9.99)
30 Things Future Dads Should Know About Pregnancy
(ISBN: 9781596525924, $9.99)
33 Things To Know About Raising Creative Kids
(ISBN: 9781596525627, $9.99)
34 Things To Know About Wine
(ISBN: 9781596525894, $9.99)